Men to Run From

So You Can Find the Right One to Run To

**"Wise, Witty, Warm, and Insightful,
This Gem Of a Guide Helps Women
Understand How Men Think and Behave**
Catherine Cardinal's clear and funny prose helps readers better
understand their guy, themselves, and what it takes to build a
loving, long-term relationship."

—PAMELA HOGAN, PhD,
author of *Keep Your Relationship, Keep Your Self:
Men and Women, Making Peace & Making Love*

"Look no further! *Men to Run From* is a brilliant book about the
men we think we want, the men we really want, and every type
of man in between."

—ERIN KAMLER,
author and composer of *Divorce! The Musical*

"Cardinal has an ability to explore the complex subject of
relationships with clarity and wit. Her years of expertise,
insightful observations, and tell-it-like-it-is approach make this
an essential book for anyone facing the challenges of dating and
relationships today."

—BONNIE CURTIS,
producer of *Saving Private Ryan*

"Catherine has given us a simple, perceptive and humorous
account of the male species and how they behave. If only I'd
read this book twenty years ago, I would have been spared
immeasurable heartbreak."

—VICKI SWANSON, MA, DC,
developer of "Conscious Exercise" seminars

**"Men to Run From May Single-Handedly Launch
A Million Happy Marriages!**
Finally, someone has broken down the complicated world of men and
relationships into an easy-to-understand and entertaining book.

Every woman needs this book, and probably every man
should read it, too."

—JAN JANZEN,
author of *Getting off the Merry-Go-Round:
How to Create the Life You Want
Without the Fear, Doubt and Guilt*

"Catherine Cardinal's wonderful book made me laugh out loud.
She's funny and she's wise. Heed her advice!"

—JULIA COHEN,
Professor of Psychology, Pierce College, Los Angeles

"As a singer and songwriter, I know a lot of songs about heartache
and bad breakups. Thank God for Catherine, whose wise book
helps women meet great guys rather than the kind who inspire
woeful ballads. I hear her voice when I read each chapter, and it
makes me smile."

—KELLY HARPER,
singer/songwriter, best known for "New Best Friend"
No. 38 on Top 40, Contemporary Hit Radio

"What a wonderful book! I wish I had read it when I was younger
and still on the hunt for a good, solid mate! It would have helped
tremendously, because I think I dated every single one of the
twenty types of 'Men to Run From' depicted in your book."

—SUZANNE MATHIS, editor

"This Light-Hearted Yet Insightful Book Will Help You to Leap Past The Frogs And Into the Arms of a Real Prince. When it comes to choosing a man, the more food for thought the better.

In that respect, *Men to Run From* is a sumptuous dessert."

—KRISTINA WAYBORN,
who played a Bond girl in *Octopussy*, and
who acted on *The Love Boat*, *Dallas*,
Baywatch, and *General Hospital*

"Insightful and humorous! Dr. Cardinal's book is clear, compelling, and concise. I am confident this easy-to-read and indispensable manual will benefit men and women."

—DR. ANDRE BERGER,
medical director and founder of
Rejuvalife Vitality Institute, Beverly Hills, CA

"*Men to Run From* gives women valuable information about men and their behaviors, which can only lead to better relationship choices. Every woman will benefit from knowing what category her man falls into, and can then decide whether to run away or follow her expert advice."

—JULIE SPIRA,
best-selling author, *The Perils of Cyber-Dating:
Confessions of a Hopeful Romantic
Looking for Love Online.*

ALSO BY CATHERINE CARDINAL, PhD

A Cure for the Common Life:

The Cardinal Rules of Self-Esteem

Men to Run From

So You Can Find the Right One to Run To

Written by Catherine Cardinal, PhD

Illustrated by Marco Arcipreste

Edited by Gali Kronenberg

New York

Men to Run From

So You Can Find the Right One to Run To

Edited by Gali Kronenberg
Illustrated by Marco Arcipreste

ISBN 978-1-60037-597-2

Library of Congress Control Number: 2009922065

MORGAN · JAMES
THE ENTREPRENEURIAL PUBLISHER

Morgan James Publishing, LLC
1225 Franklin Ave., STE 325
Garden City, NY 11530-1693
Toll Free 800-485-4943
www.MorganJamesPublishing.com

In an effort to support local communities, raise awareness and funds, Morgan James Publishing donates one percent of all book sales for the life of each book to Habitat for Humanity. Get involved today, visit **www.HelpHabitatForHumanity.org.**

*To John-- My lighthouse. My friend. My lover. My husband.
You have won my heart. Thank you for showing me
it's never too late to find true love.*

*And to my many incredible clients... you continue to be my
most-treasured teachers.*

And to Fred...thanks for everything.

"No boy is worth crying over,
and the one who is won't make you cry."
—Sarah Kane, age 10[*]

Contents

Foreword

So many of us end up with relationship problems that we just didn't see coming. That's how I met Catherine, who helped me after a bad break-up. I mean, no one goes into a relationship thinking, "Well, this guy is sure to crush my spirit and break my heart."

Yet it happens. It's happened to me.

And half the battle with me after a breakup is beating myself up, which is why I'm now in favor of arranged marriages. At least if my mom picks the guy and it goes completely awry, I won't have to sit in a bean bag chair with a bottle of Scotch for six months wondering, "What the hell is wrong with me?" Instead, I can just look over at my mom and say, "You did it again!"

The truth is, before I met Catherine and heard her clear, compassionate, and practical advice, I'd languish in a bad relationship for years and suffer. No matter if the awful relationship was with an agent, manager, publicist, or boyfriend, the Midwestern girl in me said, "He's a good guy. He's trying. He hasn't done anything that horrible."

That's how low I'd set the bar.

I simply did relationships old-school, Irish style. You suck it up, have another beer, and let him watch his football, until one day, when it becomes too unbearable, you walk out.

If only I'd read *Men to Run From: So You Can Find the Right One to Run To* years ago, I could have saved myself a lot of pain and anguish. Then again, as a comic, I would have lost a solid ten minutes of really good material from my act.

While reading *Men to Run From*, I started recognizing all of these types of men I'd dated, and I would yell aloud, "Damn, how did I miss that?"

I guess that's the benefit of Catherine's years of experience and her insights into relationships. She knows how to help you spot where things are headed early on and how to correct course or, if needed, jump ship. Having read her book, I think I finally got it, though the answer came to me in the form of an Irish nautical metaphor:

Better to learn how to spot a seaworthy vessel in port than to spend years bailing water from a sinking ship.

This is why I firmly believe that *Men to Run From* should be given to every woman upon college graduation. Hey, while you're in college, you should still be allowed to date anyone. You want to date the idiot? Go ahead. You want to sleep with the hot jock who will never call you again? Fine. But after college, you should have this book handed to you along with your diploma. The book will only take a short while to read, but it can save you years of regret, confusion, and pain.

Catherine Cardinal has spent a lifetime listening and giving wise counsel. Take her advice!

—Kathleen Madigan

Madigan is a regular guest on *The Tonight Show with Jay Leno, The Late Show with David Letterman, Light Night with Conan O'Brien,* VH-1, E!, CNN, and Comedy Central. She is also the talent scout on NBC's *Last Comic Standing* and a writer and comic on the new series *Lewis Black's Root of All Evil.*

Acknowledgments

To my editor, Gali Kronenberg—it's truly rare to meet someone like you. Thank you for enriching this book with your genius, insight, and amazing fluency and talent with words. Beyond the manifold ways you elevated my language and ideas, you shared with me your gift for drawing out the best in people and inspired me to do my best work. I love you, you're brilliant!

To my illustrator, Marco Arcipreste—with a few strokes of your pen, you made my characters come to life! Thank you for your artistic talent, your dedication, and great sense of humor. Your artwork truly helps to complete this book.

To Daniel Bushnell—thank you for being such a dear friend over all these years. You are always there when I need you. And thank you so much for introducing me to both Gali Kronenberg and Morgan James Publishing.

To Julia and Lucy Cohen—I will always treasure those afternoons I sat with you both at your kitchen table, eating snacks and listening to your feedback and suggestions for this book. You are both so clever. Where would I be without the Cohens?

A special thank you to Tom Brennan, Gary Peattie, Kathleen Madigan, Abigail Lewis, John Mallon, Lynn Marks, Dr. Vicki Swanson, and Rita Czech. A special thank you to Jason Brown for your colorful cover design and Ron Hamad for the great photo. You are both very talented.

To David Hancock and Morgan James Publishing—thank you for believing in my project and helping to bring it to life. I'm excited to be part of your vision team and look forward to our future collaborations.

Introduction

The intention of this book is to help women identify men who are great relationship material. Too many women waste far too much time in relationships that have little chance for success. To be sure, there's much about men that is mysterious, and part of the pleasure and challenge of a relationship is the unknown, the unfolding journey with one's partner.

Yet still, a good deal is knowable early on in a relationship, at least for women who become expert at identifying the male species' mating habits, behaviors, and attitudes. These women learn to pass over guys who, for a variety of reasons, are unable or uninterested in commitment and intimacy and instead focus on men who are the most capable of building and nurturing loving and long-lasting relationships.

Inspired by the National Audubon Society's *Field Guide to Birds,* with its pictures and detailed notes on avian mating habits, habitat, and so on, this book is a field guide to men; a practical MANual for recognizing red-flag men. Just as an ornithologist can distinguish the warbler from a ruby-throated hummingbird, women need to learn to discern the telltale signs of *The Wannabe; The C'mere, Go Away Guy;* and *Mr. Lives in Pictures,* among other types of men whose behavior will lead to neither long-lasting nor fulfilling relationships.

Men to Run From also encourages women to recalibrate and refine the types of men they are looking for and to take responsibility for their mating choices. This book will help you differentiate between a good choice and a poor one, and help you gain greater clarity about your relationship patterns. That's key, because recognizing the types of men you become involved with can help you to make more informed decisions.

But most of all, this book is designed to help you decide when to make the effort and work on the relationship and when to simply cut your losses and get out.

Hindsight is often our greatest teacher, and *Men to Run From* comes from my many years of hearing again and again stories about women who have spent months, often years, on men who from the outset showed every sign that they were simply not relationship material. This is why I think it is so crucial for women to learn to spot which men lack the disposition, desire, and the DNA to make a relationship work.

I prefer that women put their time and effort into relationships with viable futures rather than those that from the beginning seem destined to end badly.

Just as the *Field Guide to Birds* has pictures and profiles of varied species, these pages are filled with short profiles of the key traits of twenty types of men to avoid. Of course, many desirable guys will exhibit only some of these traits, so I remind readers that there are shades of gray within every type. One *Golden Boy*, for example, might reflect this type at its worst, while another *Golden Boy* only displays a minimum of symptoms. The point is that the latter type might still qualify as relationship material. So even if your *Golden Boy* has issues, I offer practical tips on how to strengthen your relationship so you can avoid letting those become a major problem.

Once you understand your guy more completely, you're better equipped to help steer the relationship in a healthy direction or understand why you need to end it.

By design, this book is written in an informal tone. It's easy to follow, and as you read it and share it with friends, you'll enjoy identifying which of your girlfriends is with a *Microscope Man* or *The Kid in a Candy Store*.

At the conclusion of each chapter is a section with questions to ask yourself that are designed to help you assess your situation and helpful hints on how to make it work if you are still committed to dating this type of man.

It is also likely that to one degree or another, the men in your life might exhibit traits of more than one type. This is common, because each of us embodies a variety of traits, some more dominant than others. You might find new insights about your guy in multiple chapters.

For clarity and ease of use, each chapter includes a brief summary of each of these key types of men:

- ◈ **Personality.** *What they look and sound like.*
- ◈ **Attractiveness.** *Why we are drawn to them.*
- ◈ **Challenges.** *Obstacles you will surely face with this type.*
- ◈ **Helpful Hints.** *Questions to ask yourself and things to do.*

A word to men who are reading this book: I acknowledge that I could have just as easily written a book titled *Women to Run From.* I know you go through heart-wrenching experiences too and I deeply empathize with you. I know you are searching for women who have the skills to create and sustain strong relationships. *Believe me, I know, women can have issues too!* Perhaps that will be another book, but as a woman who has heard the stories of hundreds of women, this particular guide feels like the logical place to start.

I also wish to note that while the stories throughout the book depict the relationships of heterosexual couples, it has been my experience that these insights are just as applicable to gay and lesbian couples as they are to straight ones.

Just as a savvy bird watcher can spot a rare and distinctive bird that the rest of us overlook, my desire is that this information helps you to spot that special man with whom you can build a safe, nurturing, and loving nest.

I urge you to take heart. There are many great men out there. It took me a while, but I am married to one of them. I wish you all the best on your journey.

Note: All of the names in this book have been changed to protect the privacy of the individuals.

1. The Artiste

Personality

I love creative people, don't you? The world is most certainly enriched by the presence of artists, musicians, actors, directors, and writers. At their best, their paintings, songs, plays, films, and books provoke our sense of wonder, make us laugh, weep, or recognize our common humanity.

But there is a certain type of artist who might not be the best choice for a relationship. He is consumed by his art. His time, brain, heart, and ego are wrapped up in it. His art is his mistress, not you, and he'll never treasure you the way he does his creations. This type of artist I've dubbed *The Artiste*.

The Artiste is obsessed with his work, and he doesn't have much time left for anyone else. These guys are emotionally stingy in the sense that they're so involved with themselves and their art that they're unable to cherish, be attentive, be affectionate, or be deeply interested in their partners.

Monica, an old friend of mine, found me on Facebook and we re-connected. I was excited to see her and invited her over for lunch.

When she arrived at my home, she looked sad and tired. After our 'girlfriend to girlfriend catch-up', tuna salads and a glass of wine, the story of Monica and her current boyfriend of two years, Michael, spilled out. They were sharing a beach house in Venice and clearly, things were not going well.

"Michael is a musician, a composer," she began. "I instantly fell for him. He's handsome and talented and all the women love him. I felt so lucky to get him to even notice me.

"From the start, he made it clear that his music was more important than I was, but at least back then he tried to please me. That lasted about four months. Then he started spending more and more time in his studio and less and less time with me. I would beg him to spend ten minutes with me, and he'd say, 'I have to get back to my music. You simply don't understand.'"

Monica burst out into tears. "I do understand!" she cried. "I want to be understanding. I bring his meals to him in his studio which is in the back of our place. I invite a friend to join me when Michael is too busy composing to attend a function with family or friends. I even attended my cousin's wedding by myself. Most nights, Michael works until three or four in the morning, so I usually go to bed by myself. I don't complain.

"But the more space I give him the more he wants. It bothers me, but I keep thinking that if I am patient and understanding, things will get better. After all his music is his work."

I knew from what Monica was telling me, things would probably not get better. I wanted to help her as I have heard this "Artiste" story many times before, but she actually had to run by this time for another commitment. I hugged her, encouraging her to take care of herself and listen to her inner wisdom. We promised to get together when I got back from a business trip I had lined up.

About two weeks later Monica called me and told me she was leaving Michael. It seems Michael had become close to another female musician and they were spending quite a bit of time together. One particular evening, Monica returned home around midnight, having spent the evening with her sister, and found Michael in the studio, alone with his new friend Caitlyn. The room was dark except for a candle.

Monica said loudly, "Hey! What's going on in there?" Michael responded, "Sshhh! Caitlyn and I are listening to the acoustic track I just laid down." Monica was stunned. She told me, "I couldn't believe it! This woman was in my house, sitting next to my boyfriend at midnight, in the dark and he was shushing me!"

It was at this point that Monica knew the relationship was over. I was thrilled.

The following week Monica and I met for lunch in Brentwood and she told me, "The surprising part was that

Michael was genuinely shocked when I left. He cried and kept saying, 'I care for you, how can you leave me?' I knew he was oblivious to how badly he had treated me and I felt kind of sad for him. I also knew he was wondering how anyone could leave the great composer."

Monica's story is a classic example of how *The Artiste* journeys through life. The lyrics to the soundtrack of his life go something like this: "Stand back. Stand back. Only women who wish to be my muse, helper, or audience need apply."

Creating art is not easy. Neither are these men.

Attractiveness

The Artiste can be intriguing, and these men often have enormous appeal and charisma. Art comes from within and can touch the heart and soul. These are the parts we most yearn to have touched! We are often seduced by this guy's sensitivity, his creative ability, and the seeming depth of his soul. We are sure that the tenderness he lavishes on his art will eventually be given to us.

Of course, many men are both creative and self-aware. These guys understand balance, and for them, intimacy and love nourish their work. They may make sacrifices for their art, but they can also dedicate themselves to a relationship, marriage, and children. If you find a guy like this, good for you! Such men can be very loving, playful, and fun. This is a man to run to!

Challenges

If you're willing to play second fiddle to his art, then you'll have few problems. He might not have a lot of time for you, and if you have plans for a romantic dinner or a night out with friends, and inspiration strikes, he will likely bow out to work on his current creation. You might start to feel as if you're in competition with his painting, novel, or sonata.

I recall a scene from *Sex in the City* in which Carrie is dating a Russian artist. There is a party being thrown in Carrie's honor, but the artist makes it clear that he needs her by his side at his art opening. To be a good partner, Carrie passes up her own party to accompany him. Once there, he disappears to schmooze with the press and his public, and Carrie is left utterly alone in a crowded room. She sacrificed her own event, and he neglected to spend time with her or introduce her to his friends.

Helpful Hints
Important questions to ask yourself:

1. Does he have balance in his life? Does he make time for you, exercise, and meals, or is most of his time devoted to his art?
2. Does he take an interest in your interests, and is he available to meet your emotional and social needs?
3. Is it more important for him to spend time with other artists than to spend time with you, or is he able to do both?

Things to Do

This guy needs balance. Working on his art is a kind of high for him. It feels so good that he might not want to come down, and it might cause him to lose perspective about you and the relationship.

I suggest adopting a few ground rules. For instance, set aside a designated night each week for you to enjoy dinner together, or to have a date night or evening with friends. This kind of structure can support both of you. Both of you should write it on your respective schedules at the beginning of the week to avoid confusion. This way you'll have a shared expectation as to what night he'll be free and which nights he'll be working. Artists are visual. If he sees it, he expects to take that night off, and you won't have to feel as if you're badgering him.

If he is too self-involved, your suggestions will make him feel stifled, and he'll see you as keeping him from his art. He might not even hear much of what you're saying, because he resents the demands that you're placing on him. In this case, if you choose to stay with him, you will have to work around his schedule and learn to be OK with it.

If you're not OK with that arrangement, just know that unless you can turn *The Artiste* into a mature artist, capable of balancing a relationship and work, you'd be wise to put on your ballet slippers and *sauter*, in other words, leap on out of there and exit stage right!

2. Microscope Man

Personality

This guy doesn't miss a thing! He micromanages every last aspect of his life. Everyone from colleagues to his family thinks of him as anal-retentive. His motto is, "A place for everything, and everything in its place." This includes you!

Many years ago in one of my Movement Expression Therapy classes, I remember one attendee, Patty, telling the group this story.

She loved her boyfriend Alex because he was organized and together, whereas Patty had a tendency to be scattered and unfocused. She didn't mind his chiding about her disorderly office, late credit card payments, or an out-of-place lock of hair. She thought this was his way of helping her to be a better person.

But when he started commenting on her choice of outfits, saying, "I know you love red, but it's a terrible color for you," or "That outfit makes your butt look too big," she began to feel overwhelmed by Alex's relentless perfectionism.

One morning she woke up to find him staring intently at her face. "Before saying, 'Good morning,' or asking me how I slept, he told me, 'You have a new line under your eyes, and you know your crow's feet are getting worse.'"

This is *Microscope Man* at his classic and insufferable worst. Sure, we can have sympathy for him and understand that he is likely the product of an overbearing mother or critical father. Still, how many of us would want to live under his incessant, critical gaze? For him, the world must hew to his design.

Often *Microscope Man* fears his own inadequacy and compensates with perfectionism. When he spots a speck of white lint on the black shirt of life, he is quick to comment. This can happen in just about any setting, and he is notorious for making people around him feel uncomfortable and self- conscious, a bit like driving next to a cop.

But it's not his crusade against lint that I'm worried about. It's what he does to his significant other that is devastating. His nit-picking perfectionism can crush a person's sense of self and whittle away at one's sanity. It's not normal or natural to have every hair in place at all times, yet what he craves is a robotically perfect Stepford Wife.

This type of man will often marry a younger, beautiful, and immature woman with the hopes of molding her to his idea of perfection. But her lack of experience and refinement may soon grow into a tremendous annoyance to him. Before long, depending on each person's capacity for self-punishment, either he'll walk out or she will.

Attractiveness

At first, we find *Microscope Men* attractive because of their keen attention to detail. Typically, they are well-organized, impeccable dressers who seem to be on top of everything. On one level, spending time with them can make some women feel safe and secure. Like Eagle Scouts, these guys appear to be prepared for everything.

Such men are often bright and articulate. Some *Microscope Men* can be geekish and not necessarily all that poised or attractive, but, for women who prize security, these guys seem to have it all under control. In a chaotic world, a *Microscope Man* who is not excessively critical can be comforting to have around.

Challenges

It is difficult to simply relax and be yourself with a *Microscope Man*. His critical take on life can put you on edge and make you feel as if you are walking on eggshells. Though it is often on an unconscious level, these men are deeply disappointed in themselves, and before long they will project their dissatisfaction onto you. This type of guy also needs to feel in control, so don't expect spontaneity, sexual abandon, or raucous exuberance.

If you're a positive, upbeat person who perceives the glass as half full, a *Microscope Man* will be difficult to tolerate over time.

Helpful Hints
Important questions to ask yourself:

1. How often does he point out some flaw about you or the world?
2. Does he let you know that you are falling short of his standard? Are his standards so high that no matter how hard you try, you will never be good enough?
3. Does he feel uncomfortable or panicked when he isn't in control?
4. Does he get frustrated and angry when things don't go his way?

Things to Do

Microscope Man is often not even aware that he has a problem. From his perspective, the trouble is, "the damned imperfection of this world and the fools who don't get it."

First and foremost, do not allow him to criticize you. Tell him in your own words that his critiques of you are not acceptable. Let him know it makes you feel uncomfortable and that you want him to notice and tell you what he likes about you. Be clear that you value a supportive environment.

If he can start to relax and ease off on his controlling tendencies, maybe he can catch a glimpse of the perfection within the imperfection and the beauty that comes from accepting life at face value.

Control issues are difficult to change. Let your self-esteem be the barometer that tells you if it's time to go. Rule number one in my book, *A Cure for the Common Life: The Cardinal Rules of Self-Esteem* is "Don't hang around people who make you feel bad about yourself."

3. The Wannabe

Personality

If this guy wasn't a braggart, he'd probably have better luck. He hungers to be a VIP, and you want to root for him to get there, but his personality can be such a turn-off.

My friend Lisa had been dating Jack for two weeks, when they went out to eat one night and left their car with the valet. Lisa cringed when she heard Jack hand over his keys and say, "I'm Jack Smith, and I own all the villas in the Crestview development."

If that wasn't bad enough, days later she heard Jack use the same line to introduce himself to strangers at a party. Only after she broke up with him did she learn that he wasn't the owner, but rather the owner's assistant.

Grant you, a lot of folks believe one should adopt a fake-it-till-you-make-it attitude. At one time or another, we have all been wannabes, striving to meet a fresh goal and trying not to mess up too badly along the way.

This is not the type of guy I'm talking about here. I'm referring to men who are blowhards, guys who are all talk and no action. A blowhard doesn't work hard to reach his goals. He expects to be plucked from the pack and placed at the top, where he believes he rightfully belongs.

So how can you distinguish an everyday wannabe from a blowhard who sits on his duff waiting for the world to recognize his genius? For starters, consider his work ethic, talents, training, track record, and ability to work with others. *Wannabes* who are blowhards tend to have achieved far more in their minds than in real life.

A couple of years ago, I met Brian at a conference. He was in his mid-forties, working odd jobs as a salesman, but he dreamed of becoming the next Spielberg. At that point in his *Wannabe* film career, all he had ever directed were a handful of corporate videos.

Over dinner with some colleagues, Brian spoke about what a crime it was that the world hadn't seen his films. He knew that he had talent, and all he needed, he insisted, was a break. He spoke with such passion that I offered to look at his reel. Because so many of my clients are in the entertainment industry, I thought perhaps I could be of some help.

To my dismay, the reel was worse than mediocre. Sure, I could have asked someone to look at his film as a courtesy to me, but, because he was so certain his demo reel was brilliant, I figured he wasn't open to feedback. In the end, I told him it wasn't appropriate for me to ask my clients for such favors.

The Wannabe is also green with envy toward anyone who has made it. He is certain that anyone who has hit it big had a relative, friend, or mobster uncle hand them their lucky break on a silver platter. What he fails to see is how his self-importance and boasting sabotage his own shot at success.

Another version of the *Wannabe* is the *Was-a-Be*. This is the guy who may have attained a measure of success or is highly skilled in his field. Robert, who dated my close friend

Maureen, had been successful in radio in the seventies, until all the technology changed on FM. Almost overnight, he went from being in constant demand to becoming a discarded has-been. Even though he was jobless, Robert was unwilling to get another type of job because the pay was so much lower. He also was unwilling to return to school or to study a new trade. Yet he had no problem with having Maureen take care of him until he got back on his feet. Maureen was sensitive to Robert's tough patch, but, after three jobless years, she divorced him. As adults, we need to be able to cope with change and adjust. *Was-a-Bes* are likely to stay stuck, wallow in resentment and be nothing more than your 'Knight in Whining Armor!'

Attractiveness

The Wannabe can be enticing. He is often knowledgeable and passionate about his interests. His enthusiasm can be infectious, and he may have charming stories about his skills and experiences. His belief in the big things that could happen for him can be seductive. If he is recognized one day, you could be the woman who accompanied him to success, and the brass ring could be yours. This anticipation can hook you into an unrealistic situation.

Challenges

You will have to believe in this man, no matter how long it takes for him to find his niche or get back into the swing of things. You will be expected to listen to his woeful tale over and over again as he whines, "I'm so talented, and I keep getting screwed!" If you commit to sticking with him until he gets discovered or rediscovered, you'd better have the patience of a saint, the hope of a child, and the pocketbook of a Trump.

Helpful Hints
Important questions to ask yourself:

1. We all know that success is a long-term commitment, but does your guy work toward fulfilling his goal in an informed and systematic way?
2. Is there any evidence that he actually has the skills or talent to pursue his dream? Does his education, work history, or demo reel portray any record of past accomplishment?
3. If he is unable to find a job in his chosen field, is he willing to acquire new skills or to look in a more viable job arena? How long has he been out of work?
4. Does he feel envy or admiration toward people who are doing what he wishes to do? Does he have friends and colleagues, or is he a loner or lacking in social skills? Does he appear to be lost in his daydreams or locked in a state of complaint about his circumstances?

Things to Do

Believing in one another and offering mutual support are at the heart of what a relationship is all about. That said, there is little payoff to life with a blowhard *Wannabe*, or a *Was-a-Be*. If you decide to stay with this guy, you must help him set goals. For instance, tell him he needs to go on two job interviews within a certain time period or that he needs to enroll in a school to learn a new trade or attend college or graduate school. If he makes progress, reassure him. Some *Wannabes* might break through and become productive and confident partners. It's important to set a firm time limit so that you can see evidence of him making progress toward his goals. Don't give it five long years and then decide, "Gee, that was a mistake."

If your guy is stuck and shows no sign of getting unstuck, consider your own martyr/caretaker issues. A relationship is not a mutual commiseration club, and I ask you to please believe that you deserve better.

4. The Athletic Supporter

MY TEAM IS # 1

MY TEAM

Personality

Like *The Artiste* and *The Bulk Male*, *The Athletic Supporter* also has an obsession that consumes his time and loyalty. This guy spends evenings and weekends glued to his big-screen TV, watching the latest big game or perched in his seat at the stadium cheering on or cursing his team. He might play sports as well, and, in that case, on most weekends he's off hitting balls, tossing footballs, or teeing off. His conversation revolves around kick-off times, baseball scores, bad calls, replays, upcoming games, and his favorite basketball, football, soccer, golf, and baseball players. His passion for professional sports is so intense that you'd think the guys on these teams were his brothers. For him, memorizing their ranking and stats is his way of feeling a part of the team.

Attractiveness

If he is a great guy, and you share his passion for sports, you two will be fine. It's fun to have common interests with a partner, and many men appreciate it when their spouses share their interest in sports.

If he isn't just sitting on his duff watching sports, this relationship might be especially fit, energetic, and sexy. It's fun to be around passionate men who still display a boyish enthusiasm for their pursuits. I once dated a guy who loved baseball. His son was on a Little League team that he coached, and I loved going to the games with both of them.

Challenges

When thinking about being with someone who has a time-consuming passion, you must ask yourself if his lifestyle is enough of a match with your lifestyle. Depending on his sport of choice, this guy might appear to go AWOL during football or hockey season, leaving you to fill your own social calendar. The challenge is to find a compromise, cultivate your own interests, and not feel that you have lost him to sports. *Athletic Supporters* are usually up front about their love of the game. It's up to you to decide what the information means to you and your life.

Helpful Hints
Important questions to ask yourself:

1. Is the degree to which your new boyfriend is into sports going to be a problem for you? Have you thought this out? Do you think that you will change him?

2. If you are not a sports person, are you willing to get involved? If so, have you talked to him about the importance of sharing each other's interests?

3. Are you a sports widow, with a partner who has grown away from you and the relationship? Has sports filled the void in your relationship? Can you discuss this with him?

Things to Do

If you love this guy and want your relationship to work, and he is an otherwise great guy, hey, jump in and be willing to root for his team. Share in the excitement of the victory and the agony of defeat. Be prepared to attend games with him and share his joy. If that isn't you, then let him do his sports thing while you do your own thing.

You can work out a compromise. You can say, "Honey, I'll go to the big game on Sunday, but, next Saturday, let's go the beach and visit a few antique stores on the way home." If you love one another and are committed to the relationship, you can develop some give and take. I've seen many couples with disparate interests forge rich and balanced relationships.

But if he is unwilling to make an adjustment to meet you halfway, or if you feel that you are utterly ignored and that you always take a backseat to the game, it's time to check the score. If you are coming up with "I'm getting none of my needs met," you may need to consider whether this *Athletic Supporter* fits into your own game plan.

5. Boyz

Personality

Beware of *Boyz* posing as men. These guys might be youthful, playful, and charming, but unless you want to play mommy to your mate, think again. No matter the man's chronological age, this guy is why they coined the term "arrested development."

Whatever reason caused Peter Pan to never want to grow up—immature parents, dysfunctional family, a critical father or smothering mother, or his own alcohol and drug use—remember, it is one thing to raise a child and another to marry one. Don't let the charm of his youthful energy and boyish spirit fool you; the bottom line is that these lads are unable to step up or grow up.

It is important not to confuse the adult love a woman feels for a man with the maternal love a mother feels toward her child.

And that's how this guy acts—like a child. His emotional maturity can fluctuate depending on his mood or the situation.

I call the least mature of the *Boyz* the youngsters. These men, despite their outward physical maturity, are self-centered, insist on getting their way, and are unable to consider anything beyond their own needs. They think in gimme-gimme terms, and, just like little tykes, they will pout when they don't get their way. These guys might be lawyers, teachers, or mechanics; no matter their job or education level, they are still capable of throwing temper tantrums.

The thing is, these guys have a boyishness and charm that can be so darn cute! They are good at getting what they want, both from you and the world at large.

The noted Swiss psychologist Jean Piaget calls this stage of cognitive development the *pre-operational stage*. What this means is that a man in *Boyz* mode is incapable of taking into account another person's point of view. If he says, "I'm hungry right now," then he is certain that you must be hungry, too. Or, if he wants to eat a burger, then that is the best food in the whole world, and you, too, must desire a quick stop at McDonald's for a burger and fries.

In the end, he's trained you that it is easier to give in, eat the burger, go where he wants, or do something you have no interest in doing. Before you know it, your relationship isn't the adult give-and-take of a man and woman but the one-way caretaking of a mom indulging a demanding child.

Piaget dubbed the next stage of development *concrete operational*, which, for simplicity's sake, I'll call the "tweens." This guy is sophisticated enough to recognize that you too have a unique point of view, but he believes that his is more important. Such men can lack empathy. Say, for instance, you and your guy take turns picking movies on date night. On a given Friday night, it is his turn to pick the movie. But on that particular night, you have a searing headache and cramps and don't feel well enough to go out.

Your partner, in true *Boyz* fashion is still itchin' to go, and he cajoles you by saying, "We saw that chick flick you wanted to see last week. Just take some aspirin. This movie's gonna be great, and I don't want to miss it." He only knows that it's his turn and "it's not fair." He is incapable of taking care of you. All he is focused on is you thwarting him from having fun.

I refer to the next, slightly more mature, version of this group as "the teens." This guy is still self-centered and focused solely on his own needs, but he is capable of thinking in abstract terms. He can have flashes of empathy and even recognize that there is more than his wants to consider, yet he can remain obsessed by what ought to be rather than what is. The result is that when he is faced with a situation that conflicts with what he wants, he's easily frustrated, riled up, or overwhelmed.

For instance, this guy feels hassled by his boss. He's convinced he's unappreciated, unfairly singled out, and overworked for too little pay. One day he blows up, fights with his boss, and walks out with no other job possibilities. If you show any sign of worry as to how the two of you will cover the bills, you become a traitor. His response is, "You're never on my side; you don't respect me. You're just like everyone else."

It's too nuanced, too adult for him to understand that you could a) really love and support him, b) also be concerned about how to pay the mortgage, and c) be peeved that he didn't try to look for a new job before quitting his old one.

No matter which type they are, *Boyz* are simply unable to behave in an adult manner, and an adult discussion of issues will fly over their heads.

Due to my caretaker nature, I have been involved with a few *Boyz*. A part of me once believed that the more I cared for this type of man and met his every need, the more he would love me and meet my needs. This is absolutely *not* true. To avoid feeling hurt, angry, and resentful, adult relationships require a mutual desire to meet each other's needs.

Attractiveness

These guys have the cute, charming, adorable thing going for them. They are often boyishly good looking with winning smiles. They really know how to work their charm and can be irresistible. Whatever their age, they are often endearing. Even as adults, they can exude the adorableness of David Archuletta or the sexy, misunderstood poutiness of James Dean.

These men are playful, and it's easy to feel smitten with them. But be cautioned, this isn't merely an adult who is youthful, fun, and childlike; this could be an adult hiding in a self-centered, childish mind.

Challenges

Ladies, these guys are tough, tough, tough to deal with. They have great difficulty in acknowledging anything beyond their own needs and can't differentiate reality from the way they wish it to be. One client dated a guy who was wild about her until he heard her use the bathroom. He said that that alone made him lose all attraction to her. These *Boyz* can be unpredictable and emotionally brutal. Ever watch kids on a playground?

Boyz often act like spoiled, demanding, narcissistic children. Unless the relationship matures, these guys can leave you feeling as exhausted as if you were running a daycare.

Helpful Hints:
Important questions to ask yourself

1. Does he insist on his way more than seems fair and equitable?
2. Is he prone to whining, sulking, tantrums, or bouts of anger when things don't go his way?
3. Do you find yourself taking care of him and making sure his needs are met at the expense of your own? Are you telling yourself that if you take care of him, he will eventually grow up and be your perfect partner?
4. Are you content to be with *Boyz* because you feel like a kid yourself? If so, is someone taking care of life's daily details and making sure the wolf won't be at the door? Can you assume that responsibility without growing resentful?
5. If you are attracted to the bad-boy type with a Kurt Cobain living-on-the-edge sensibility, are you really able to create and sustain a stable relationship?

Things to Do

If you feel fulfilled taking care of and mothering him, this relationship can work. If playing the adult in the relationship allows you to set boundaries that he respects, then things might work out fine for both of you. After all, kids are refreshing and fun. I have seen this kind of partnering, and it can be successful. It's only when you are filling a role that you are not comfortable with that problems arise. Only you can determine if this kind of relationship is right for you.

If you want this relationship to work, recall what parents do to get results from a child. Yelling is rarely helpful. He will only tune you out and grow to hate you. Create a system of rewards for his grown-up behavior and consequences for his childish behavior.

But if mothering is not for you, this relationship will grow tiresome and frustrating. He needs to make the leap into manhood, but there isn't much you can do to make this happen. It usually happens as a result of some outside influence; it's his personal journey. Even if he does happen to make this leap while with you, he often will leave. One of the things I have seen with women—and I've been in this situation myself—is that when *Boyz* become men, they discover the need to leave home. It is the natural order of things. So be cautious that you are not helping to guide one of these *Boyz* into manhood just to make him capable of a more mature relationship with another woman.

If you happen to get hurt by one of these juvenile men, don't take it personally. Just know that he lacks what it takes to see the best in you. Unless you have a driving urge to play mom to your partner, give him up for adoption and find yourself a grownup.

6. The Salesman

Personality

This guy might be a salesman by trade, but, whatever his career, the thing he is selling is an inflated, hyped, improved version of himself. *Salesman* types come in many shades, from the modest embellisher to the hard-core con artist.

The more innocent version is simply a guy with weak self-esteem who talks a good story to make himself look like a winner. He'll promise you a new car, a bigger house, a dream vacation; whatever it takes to convince you he's a "somebody" who is worthy of dating.

Of course, the cost of such behavior is that when the truth comes out, you lose all trust in him and are left wondering who this man is that you're dating.

A friend of mine, Karen, couldn't wait for me to meet her new boyfriend, Larry. My first impression was that Larry, a computer consultant, was a delight. He was a great storyteller, and all of us at the table fell madly in love with him!

Over the next ten months, Karen would call me from time to time, crying about Larry. Little by little, she had discovered holes in his stories, and his bio no longer seemed to add up. She now felt certain that he had never been a marine, attended Yale, or was set to inherit a hefty sum of money. Who was this man she was dating? When she confronted him, Larry broke down and admitted that he had embellished a few things about his past. But, he insisted, he had only done it to please her. Karen assured him his half-truths and deceptions had done anything but please her.

She felt betrayed and lost all trust in him. Larry was remorseful for his actions, and though he had some wonderful qualities, Karen opted to move on. Years later, I heard that Larry was happily involved with another woman. Perhaps, chastened by his experience with Karen, he was able to change.

At the other end of the spectrum is a *Salesman* who is simply a con artist and the kind of guy you should run from and not give a second thought to trying to rehabilitate. Don't be naïve; this guy views you more as an easy mark than as his girlfriend. Let me be clear, this type of man is a scam artist who preys on women. The way to recognize him is if you've only been going out a short time and he suggests that you a) loan him money, b) sign on a dotted line, or c) help him with his surefire, get-rich scheme that only requires a modest investment on your part.

If he conned you with his charm, don't beat up on yourself. This guy became a *Salesman* because he comes across as believable. His motive isn't to win you over because he feels insecure. His plan is to hoodwink you, steal as much as he can from you, and skip town.

Attractiveness

On the charm scale, *The Salesman* is usually off the chart. *Salesmen* are smooth, charismatic, and very believable. They are stuck in the stage where they first learned how to get what they wanted by lying, and by their current age they are good at it. Most children outgrow this phase, but, in *The Salesman's* case, either poor parenting or arrested development caused him to stay in this mind-set.

The Salesman is typically a charmer, and whether he is genuinely successful or not, he appears to be.

Challenges

With the more extreme *Salesmen*—the liars, cheaters, stealers, and swindlers—the challenges are more than anyone should tolerate.

The mild embellisher, who is covering up low self-esteem to feel better about himself, might be in your range of manageability. The main challenge will be discerning when he's being totally honest, telling a little white lie, or being completely deceitful. If he seems to stay primarily in the range of embellishment and little white lies, you might decide it's workable. If all of your other needs are being met, you might want to stay. There are many men who are worse than a harmless teller of tall tales.

Helpful Hints
Important questions to ask yourself:

1. Does he have lots of great stories and make big promises early in the relationship? Are you in awe of him? Are you staying in touch with your intuition?

2. Do all of his stories match? Is there ever a time where you say to yourself, "This story was different the last time I heard it"?

3. Does he seem to invent bigger and better stories to match the situation that you're in?

4. Is he asking you for loans or for money to invest? Is he asking questions about your assets, salary, savings, et cetera?

Things to Do

The only *Salesman* worthy of your time and energy is the mild embellisher. Keep reaffirming how important the truth is to you, and that you love him for who he is. Help build his self-esteem through positive encouragement, and he might release his need to impress you and others. Let him know that you love him, look in his eyes if you suspect he's embellishing, and ask, "Is that true?" In these instances, your loving support may transform him from a white liar into your white knight. If he cannot find the strength within himself to let go of these bad habits, you will have to decide if you can live with his facades.

If you are dealing with an extreme case of *The Salesman,* the thing to do is grab your purse, your integrity, your sanity, and run. Hopefully you do this before he causes you too much hurt.

These impostors always have a steady stream of women interested in them, and they have exquisitely refined radar for naïve and trusting women. I don't wish to be negative here, but, if your new guy seems to be too good, too perfect to be true, perhaps he is. Make sure you put in the time to get to know him before committing your heart.

7. The Immature, Premature Transcendent

STAND BACK !!!
I AM TUNING INTO
THE UNIVERSE...

OM...

Personality

He might have two feet, but neither of them is rooted on the ground. He is a meditating, guru-hopping, detachment-seeking, lentil-eating, soul-traveling, chakra-balancing, astral-projecting flake. This guy is all lightness and no substance.

When it comes to relationships, in spite of all of his spiritual growth, he has neglected to grow up, and despite all of his vaunted love and bliss, he is unable to sustain a committed relationship. He might have found detachment from mundane earthly preoccupations that unfortunately can include a decent job, a family, or any sense of future. He's better at loving his guru than making a relationship work with his partner.

Of course there are men out there who are on spiritual or religious paths with both feet on the ground, who make exceptional partners. These guys have great ethics, big hearts, and a serenity that comes with an authentic sense of faith. These men tend to be positive, upbeat, and they make great dads, partners, and friends. If you find such a guy, hang on to him! He's learned to balance his spiritual life with his earthly life, and he can be a loving, committed partner.

The Immature, Premature Transcendent, on the other hand, believes that human emotions get in the way of his spiritual path. For him, attachments are to be overcome, love must be unconditional, and commitment is an illusion. Sure, he'll stay in a relationship with you, but only as long as it goes with the flow. If he perceives you as impeding his spiritual growth, he will leave.

The problem with these types of seekers is that they are so heavenly, they're of no earthly good. They've made what I call "the metaphysical jump" and are missing the necessary emotional and psychological development necessary for sustaining a mature, long-term relationship.

Melanie, a friend I met while teaching at The Learning Annex, fell in love with a man she met at a meditation seminar. "Tobie has the kindest voice and the sweetest temperament," she said. "He meditates for two hours a day and spends his weekends practicing yoga and attending spiritual retreats. And he has the most amazing energy."

Melanie, who followed a similar spiritual path, was sure she had found her soul mate. For the first few months, they meditated together, walked on the beach, and attended spiritual workshops. Melanie was in heaven. She fantasized about their wedding, their children, and the spiritual retreat site that Tobie hoped to open. Melanie was 100 percent sure that it would all unfold just as she visualized, which she did daily as part of her meditation exercises.

After nine months of dating, Tobie still avoided the issue of commitment. When she'd bring it up, Tobie would say, "Spirit will tell us when it is time." Melanie, wanting to believe in divine timing, didn't push it, and she held on to her faith that it would all work out.

After a year and a half, Melanie grew more and more frustrated. When she'd discuss this with Tobie, he would say she was not being spiritual and was letting her anger swallow her serenity. "Love is unconditional," he said. "That's how the great masters love."

This confused Melanie. She was in her mid-thirties and anxious to get her family started. It was at this point that she called me for advice.

The first thing I asked her was what she felt *unconditional love* meant. She replied, "Loving people for exactly who they are with no expectations." I replied, "Regarding love, it's a beautiful concept. But in a relationship, is it realistic?" She wasn't sure what I meant.

"Do you have a condition that your marriage partner speak English?" I asked.

"Yes," she said.

"That he not be a murderer?"

"Yes."

"That he listens to you when you speak to him?"

"Yes."

"That he wants children?"

"Yes."

"That he earns an income and cares for his family?

"Yes."

She started to get my point. I told her, "Melanie, love may be unconditional, but relationships *must* be conditional. It's how we know who to marry. We marry people with similar conditions. Relationships must be conditional to work."

Considering the fifteen years that Melanie had spent on a spiritual path, this was difficult for her to come to terms with. After a few moments of silence on the phone, she said, "All this time, Tobie has been asking me to love him unconditionally in our relationship, yet that, too, is a condition. It's been conditional the entire time. It's just been his conditions. He's had everything just the way he wants it!"

This was the exact point I wanted her to see.

Melanie confronted Tobie, who after an all-night discussion, finally admitted that he was scared to death of commitment, marriage, and losing his freedom. Underneath all of the spiritual development and new-age clichés was a scared man. Melanie opted to move on, remaining good friends with Tobie.

I'm happy to say that my friend Melanie is now happily married and has two beautiful children.

Attractiveness

The most attractive aspect of these guys is their interest in the innermost world. Women are focused inward as a general rule, contemplative and reflective. A man who is able to connect to spirit or divinity can be extremely enticing.

It's not every man who takes an interest in the subtle nature of things. The two of you can enjoy sharing your spiritual journey, taking classes together, and an openhearted way of connecting. Such men often love nature, hiking, and camping, and these outings can bring a sense of renewal and can serve as a welcome antidote to the stress and strains of modern life.

A lot of these guys practice yoga, tai chi, or some other martial art, and are often fit, handsome, and have a good vibe. He no doubt enjoys talking about his spiritual inquiry, his dreams, meditations, or the teachings of the masters he's picked up from books, gurus, or seminars. We all desire love, and a guy who appears to have found some degree of inner peace and contentment can be blissful to be around.

Challenges

In one arena, *The Immature, Premature Transcendent* shares similarities with *The Artiste, Golden Boy, The Kid in a Candy Store,* and *He's a Young Thing and Cannot Leave His Mother.* In this case, however, instead of competing with his art, his ego, other women, or his mother, you're competing with God, the highest power, the top banana! It's difficult to win this one, and it can really mess with your head, causing you to feel that there is something wrong with you.

Unless you share the same level of spiritual commitment and have few other needs, this relationship will be hard on your self-esteem.

Helpful Hints
Important questions to ask yourself:

1. Does his spiritual path keep him unavailable and unwilling to be present with you in the relationship?

2. Do you find yourself questioning if you are a bad person because you have needs? Does he imply that you are too attached and needy when you feel you are asking for normal relationship interactions?

3. Is he avoiding commitment and planning for your future together? How long has this been going on?

Things to Do

Find out if there is the possibility for authentic give and take in this relationship. Be willing to make clear requests of him. For instance, in addition to his daily meditation, he needs to commit to an activity with you, perhaps taking a walk. Make it clear that the time he spends with you and the time he invests in your life as a couple is just as important as his spiritual practice. If he agrees, does he follow through?

If he starts giving you his unconditional love sermon, and can't recognize that it is OK for lovers to make commitments to one another, then it's probably best to move on. Keep in mind that reverence, kindness, and love are not abstract feelings that we reserve for God alone. They are qualities we also show our partners.

8. The Loose Cannon

Personality

This is the guy who can't control his temper. It takes very little for this volcano to erupt, and there's no way to predict what will set off his next seismic disturbance. His rage can be verbal as well as physical, and it seldom bears any sense of proportion to what angers him. One client confided that her husband had punched a hole in the wall because she had accidentally ruined his favorite shirt.

Of course, anyone can get angry, and intimacy and cohabitation—not to mention life in general—can stir up powerful emotions. *The Loose Cannon*, however, does more than simply yell, storm out of the room, or punch a pillow in a rare show of anger or frustration.

The Loose Cannon is a rage-aholic. He gets a rush from anger, which feels far better to him than depression or dealing with his inner demons on a rational basis. This is why he is always on the hunt, even if he isn't conscious of it, for something new to get angry about. Because anything under the sun has the potential to piss him off, you never know from one moment to the next if he's going to rage about the SOB who is driving too slowly, the neighbor's dog, or his idiot brother who never does anything right.

Attractiveness

The Loose Cannon can have a calm side that masks his anger. Then one day he gets upset and you see the rage underneath. In every other respect, he might seem normal. He might even have a good sense of humor, other wonderful qualities, a professional job, and be very caring. Because *The Loose Cannon* can come in any package, you might have been attracted to him for any number of reasons.

There are women who are drawn to what they view as tough men. They feel flattered by a mistaken sense of these men's chivalry or willingness to duke it out in their honor. A woman in love with a *Loose Cannon* needs to realize that one day he might duke it out with her.

Challenges

You can never predict what will anger him next, and you will run yourself ragged trying to keep things in order to prevent an outburst. Did the kids leave their bikes in the driveway? Did the dog jump up on his chair? Did someone drop by to visit without his consent? It's a very stressful way to live.

Helpful Hints
Important questions to ask yourself:

1. What percentage of the time is he angry? Does his anger seem measured or way out of proportion?
2. Are you hypervigilant and frightened? Are the kids and pets afraid of him?
3. Has he been violent? If so, have you reported him to the authorities? Has this happened more than once?

Things to Do

If this man is abusive to you, the children, or anyone close to you, get out. It is not OK to be a victim of his anger.

Do not fight him or think that you can calm him down when he is in a rage. Remove yourself and your family from the situation.

If he is not violent, and you feel that there is something to salvage in the relationship, stipulate that if he wants you to stick around, he needs to attend anger management classes or see a therapist. Without help, *Loose Cannons* can be dangerous. Unless he gets a grip on his temper and can act in a consistent, sane, and adult manner, this is definitely a guy to run from.

9. The Bulk Male

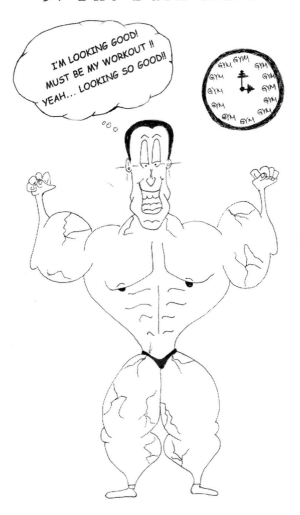

Personality

The Bulk Male is the guy who lives and breathes for his workouts at the gym. His physique is his primary focus, and his favorite topics of conversation are exercise, nutrition, and body-building. This guy shares a lot in common with *The Artiste*, but instead of art, the masterpiece that he's sculpting is his body. This guy's lair isn't his studio; he spends most of his free time at the gym.

Unless you're totally hot for the ripped physique of a bodybuilder, or you too share his pursuit of physical perfection, this might prove to be a short-lived affair.

Attractiveness

What can I say—these guys are hunks! Their hard work usually pays off, and, if you like muscled men, this guy won't disappoint. They are often disciplined and have a stick-to-itiveness that is admirable. If one of these guys is also considerate and gentlemanlike, and he holds interests outside of the gym, then he could be a good partner.

One positive payoff of the relationship could be improving your own health. You might even deepen your relationship by working out together from time to time. He and your body will appreciate it.

If he is a great guy with many wonderful qualities, you may find it worthwhile to adjust to his absence by developing your own interests. The good news with this guy is that you usually know where he is and what he's up to.

Challenges

Sharing a compatible lifestyle with someone is an important part of a balanced, fulfilling relationship. So where's your guy? If he's off lifting weights, running, riding his bike, shopping for nutritional supplements, or curled up with a muscle magazine, you might begin to feel as if you're only there for sex or to take note of his progress. Unless you're into the same level of intense training, you're likely to find the relationship limiting.

Helpful Hints
Important questions to ask yourself:

1. Are you prepared to let him focus on his workouts, or do you feel neglected and resentful?
2. Do you have any common interests, and are there things that the two of you enjoy pursuing together?
3. How important is it for him to make time for the relationship?

Things to Do

If the issue is that he spends every night at the gym or doing some athletic activity, it is vital that he is open to compromise where you both give a little, so it ends up a win-win situation.

For example, if this guy is able to work out before work or at lunch or limit his workouts to a few evenings or weekend mornings, then there's no reason his favorite pastime should pose a problem to your relationship.

What you need to ask yourself is whether or not after he is finished taking care of his health and body, he still has enough juice left to be with you.

10. The C'mere, Go Away Guy

Personality

This guy is ready and raring to woo you. He's smooth, flirtatious, and seductive. He knows how to flatter, select flowers, check in to see how your day is going, and win your heart with romance and charm.

Women with a healthy sense of self know to take things slowly and not give themselves to someone too fast. But for *The C'mere, Go Away Guy,* it is all about the ritual of pursuit and the thrill of the hunt. He will lay on the charm and mesmerize, but as soon as you are ready to respond and reciprocate by telling him that you share his feelings, he suddenly becomes cool, distant, or nonchalant. Once you fall for him, he pulls back, becomes emotionally unavailable, and might even disappear altogether.

You feel shocked, confused, and hurt. "What happened?" you ask yourself. "What did I do? Did I say something to offend him? What did I do to drive him away?" It leaves you wondering if you really knew him at all.

It's as if *The C'mere, Go Away Guy* is all dressed up but can't bring himself to actually attend the ball. Imagine a guy who decides to climb a mountain. He buys all the latest gear, works out every day, plans every detail of his ascent, but when he sees the mountain in front of him, he stops, changes his mind, and turns back around. Suddenly, he finds that the mountain that had inspired and drawn him to it requires too much commitment. The thrill had been in the preparation, the longing, the fantasy of the mountain. The actual mountain fell short.

So *The C'mere, Go Away Guy* packs up and returns home without a trace of remorse as if he had never spent weeks or months wooing you. Deep down, he knew from the outset that he'd never follow through, because he never does.

I have a dear forty-something-year-old friend, Louise, who dated a guy like this for two months. Sebastian was a gem. He was flattering, responsive, and adoring. The relationship seemed promising, and I hadn't seen Louise this optimistic about her future in years. Then one day she took the initiative to call Sebastian.

Thus far, she had enjoyed Sebastian, but he had been the one who always took the initiative to call her, make plans, or arrange for a magical night out. This was the first time she was calling him at work to say nothing more than that she was thinking of him. So when Sebastian sounded withdrawn on the call, said very little, and then didn't call her for several days, Louise didn't know what to make of it. When they finally spoke, he told her that he thought she was too needy and that he didn't want to date a woman who badgered him.

The Louise I know was neither of these things, and I couldn't fathom anything that she might have done to deserve such a response. She had been the one taking things slow. It was Sebastian's persistence that led her to feel that his affection was real, something to be trusted. This is how *C'mere, Go Away Guy* operates. In a heartbeat he can morph from warm and seductive to cold, even vicious.

Some men who fall into *The C'mere, Go Away Guy* category flirt and court women out of a need to bolster their low sense of self-esteem. This guy's behavior brings to mind Groucho Marx's quip: "I don't want to belong to any club that will accept me as a member." Once you let this guy in the door and show your love for him, he pulls away. To his way of thinking, if you love him, you must be flawed. In the end, he can only love a woman who won't love him back. Sadly, this version of *C'mere, Go Away Guy* remains trapped in a cycle of self-loathing.

Attractiveness

The C'mere, Go Away Guy is often charming, attentive, and an expert at making you feel wonderful and appreciated. They are so deft and thoughtful when courting, it's easy to see why we imagine they'd make wonderful partners. Because of their intense love of the hunt, they lure us in and we are smitten before we have a chance to realize that they might not be in it for the long haul.

These men are easy to fall in love with, and they draw women in with the greatest of ease.

Challenges

The C'mere, Go Away Guy is a dating machine. He's romantic, flirtatious, and courteous. Compliments flow from his tongue. The challenge is to move slowly so that you have enough information to weed out a *C'mere, Go Away Guy* from a true romantic who is a keeper.

If your guy falls into a pattern of splitting abruptly and then returns with apologies, be wary of his intentions. His coming back is not a sign that he is cured. I had a friend who was with a *C'mere, Go Away Guy* for nineteen years. They had their on-again time when he would be with her, but then he would inevitably retreat when she least expected it, only to return again. In their nearly two decades together, he had left twelve times. Each time, she felt elated when he came back and devastated when he left. She had become his pet yo-yo, yet she was unable to leave. After he finally left for good, she learned he had been stringing along several other women through this type of on-again, off-again relationship.

The best safeguard with any man you're unsure about is to move slowly. Take your time when dating a great guy. If he's for real, you will have a lifetime to spend together, and if he's not, you won't be as deeply hurt. Men with pathologies who pretend to be someone other than who they are tend to slip up. If you're paying attention, you'll pick up clues as to how this type of guy operates.

Helpful Hints
Important questions to ask yourself:

1. If you have met someone you feel absolutely great about, are you taking it slow? Is his affection consistent and sustained over time? Do you know that it takes at least nine to twelve months to know if someone is able to be true to his initial intention?
2. Do you know anything about his history? Has he had successful long-term relationships?
3. Does he withdraw when you show your feelings? Are his actions and emotions inconsistent? Do you beg him to stay and not go away again?

Things to Do

Remember, men fall in love over time. A guy who is too quick to profess his love might be insincere. This is not to say that if you meet a wonderful man, distrust him. But lasting intimacy and relationships with depth are about sustained affection. Don't give away your heart to the first guy who whistles.

If your wonderful new boyfriend seems like he might be the one, try to learn something about his relationship history. One way some women take stock of a *C'mere, Go Away Guy* is by getting inside information from his friends, family, or ex-girlfriends. Someone who might care about your welfare and be willing to alert you to the string of heartbroken women he has left in the dust.

Most importantly, if you are hurt by one of these meat grinders, know that it is not you. I repeat, it is not your fault if you fell for him. But if you see that he can't be there for you, say good-bye and move on with dignity.

11. The Golden Boy

Personality

This man is certain he's a prince and expects to be treated as such. He has been raised to believe that he is special, and that means that he is more special than you are. A wonder child who was adored, praised, and pampered by a parent, grandparent, teacher, or coach, this guy grew up feeling certain he was extraordinary.

Certain cultures prize male offspring, and none more so than the first-born son, but *Golden Boys* exist within all cultures.

Some *Golden Boys* anoint themselves, a reward they claimed for having achieved success at an early age. I knew a guy, James, who at twenty had landed a senior position at an entertainment company, a spot that for years had been filled by someone far older. He was rapidly promoted to still loftier perches, and when I met him, though only in his mid-thirties, James possessed a hallowed job, a hilltop home in Malibu, and scads of money. However, while James was brilliant at his work, he was incapable of maintaining a long-term relationship.

In James's mind, he was all a woman could hope for. Any woman who challenged his omniscience was out. No one, he seemed to feel, was his equal or was suitably worthy.

Of course, the problem isn't that a man is successful, intelligent, or accomplished. The trouble with *Golden Boys* is that they are conceited, intolerable, and condescending. Such men crave praise the way a drunk craves a bottle of booze. Though career success might have made him a star, I regret to say that a *Golden Boy* doesn't like to share the spotlight. He is unlikely to cast you as his leading lady, but he is happy to allow you to play a supporting role.

Attractiveness

If this *Golden Boy* description fits your man, believe me, I understand the allure. I once dated a well-educated and accomplished guy who ran an extremely successful investment firm. *Golden Boys* tend to have a lot going for them, and this one was no exception. He was bright, confident, and witty. We ate at great restaurants and attended film premiers and lavish charity benefits. But after several months, I couldn't help noticing that in social situations he always had to be the center of attention. He'd carry on about his latest business coup, his fondness for competitive skiing, and his Ferrari 550. I felt less like his girlfriend and more like an accessory. In the end, his ego overshadowed his many other charms.

Not all *Golden Boys* have scads of money. One of my colleagues, Maggie, dated a *Golden Boy* who wasn't financially well off, but he ran a major nonprofit company and was considered a highflier in their community. Maggie enjoyed their lifestyle: the fundraisers, galas, and other perks that came with her boyfriend's job. She had no trouble letting him be the star, and not long ago Maggie called to say she and her boyfriend were engaged.

Golden Boys need to flaunt their success. If you're willing, like Maggie, to play head cheerleader, such a guy can be a great match.

Challenges

Golden Boys require the spotlight. For women who are happy to be defined by a successful man, the relationship can work. But any woman who wishes to be seen as a prize in the relationship might find her self-esteem eroded. If you're dating a *Golden Boy*, it's up to you to determine if there's enough value in the relationship for you to stay.

With many *Golden Boys*, the old adage, "What goes up, must come down" applies. Some female clients have told me sad stories of once-successful men who hit rock bottom. If an unskilled, not so bright *Golden Boy* did well with daddy's money, or was just plain lucky once, it is possible that failure will overwhelm him. Like a meteor, a guy with a false and inflated sense of greatness will crash and burn.

Helpful Hints
Important questions to ask yourself:

1. Does your *Golden Boy* meet enough of your needs for you to stay in the relationship?

2. Is your *Golden Boy's* success, or potential success, based on solid ground? Tough times can happen to anyone. How would your guy cope with the loss of his job or a downturn in the stock market?

3. Is he so arrogant or full of himself that he embarrasses you in public? If so, can you cope with this?

4. How does the relationship make you feel about yourself? Do you feel stifled, oppressed, or depressed? How does it affect your self-esteem? Are your talents, opinions, and feelings recognized?

Things to Do

Sometimes *Golden Boys* are so accustomed to being the center of attention that they're mystified when someone finds them annoying.

Praising him might help to make him feel more secure, which allows you to begin to assert your own value and importance. Ask him to participate in things that are important to you. Persistence, compassion, and a little assertiveness can go a long way. Consider telling him, "Honey, I really need you to acknowledge my importance to you, and not just when we're alone, but when we're out in public." Perhaps, with gentle nudging, he can make a shift.

If you are thinking of marrying a *Golden Boy*, take note of his abilities. When you are focused on having a successful husband and financial security, then at least marry a *Golden Boy* with the drive and talent to provide for his family if the going gets tough.

If you feel the relationship is worth working on, then give it your best shot. Your *Golden Boy* might transform into a wonderful man who is willing to share center stage. There's a fine line, though, between loving and praising him and encouraging arrogant behavior. Be careful not to sacrifice too much of yourself. If you can get *Golden Boy* to feel about you the way he feels about himself, this can be an outstanding relationship.

12. The Kid in a Candy Store

I WANT THAT ONE ! ...
AND THAT ONE !...
I WANT THEM ALL !!!

Personality

This guy has an insatiable appetite for life. For him, life is one big smorgasbord, and he wants to make certain he doesn't miss out on a single treat. He is grabby, hungry, and horny.

The Kid in a Candy Store's cravings are not limited to new sexual opportunities. This guy lusts after all kinds of new experiences.

Like a child, he is drawn to all things shiny and new. It could be a car, a watch, a suit, or a trip to Las Vegas. He always has an itch to scratch, and his reasoning is clouded by desire.

On the plus side, he possesses a great *joie de vivre* and is full of passion and spontaneity. But to his detriment, no matter if his age is thirty, forty-five, or sixty, his emotional age might be closer to that of a seven-year-old who ceaselessly demands attention and the excitement of acquiring new people or things.

The Kid in a Candy Store is as easy to recognize as any other little boy. He's the one making a spectacle of himself. Often a slave to trends or a willing victim of advertising in men's magazines, he has the latest high-tech gadgets and designer duds. Whatever the newest, latest thing is, he's simply got to have it!

While most of these guys are always in pursuit of a variety of new objects or experiences, one more narrowly defined type is only after one thing—sexual variety.

This sub-type, which I call *Slick Willy*, usually reveals his intentions on the first date. He's the guy with the sexual innuendoes, the wandering hands, or the creep who slips you the tongue on your first kiss.

In short, *Slick Willy* is lecherous, and no matter how romantic or charming he seems, he has only one thing in mind: getting laid. Unless you're as sexually compulsive as Samantha from *Sex in the City*, *Slick* is not for you.

But as noted, the typical *Kid in a Candy Store* man is motivated by more than mere sex. For these guys, sameness is a kind of slow death. Unlike *Slick Willy*, he's not only fantasizing about some woman's breasts or behind, he's imagining how neat it might be to date a different kind of woman, say a flight attendant or an Asian woman, or how adventurous life might be if he dated a ballerina who travels through Europe.

This is the guy for whom the term *instant gratification* was coined. For him, relationships become tarnished over time. So unless you can reform him and he learns to cherish what he has versus what he longs for, you might find him provoking an urge within you to throw the bum out!

Attractiveness

At his best, *The Kid in a Candy Store* is fun, adorable, flirtatious, and, if true to type, really good in bed. In the beginning, you might find his curiosity, zest for life, and boyish sense of wonder exciting and endearing. When you are his new thrill, he will be attentive, adoring, and quite playful. As for *Slick Willy*, he's only charming if you're just as into one-night stands or recreational sex as he is.

Challenges

There are many. Once you are no longer *The Kid's* fresh thing, getting him to appreciate you will be a lesson in futility. Either you will feel compelled to get plastic surgery to keep his interest, or you will feel insecure, hurt, and frustrated. He has a habit of rejecting whomever he is with when a new and shiny opportunity appears. His appetite might be for more than just arm candy. This guy rebels when anyone tries to place limits on him. Urges propel him, and reason eludes him. He's the one who always wants the extra scoop, one more shot, and the last dance.

In short, he has the makings of a heartbreaker, and if you entertain the notion that you are an incredible enough woman to coax him to change, we say, "Good luck!"

So either accept the long odds against getting this guy to settle down, or adopt his attitude and play! If you like flashy, trendsetting things and don't demand emotional availability, a relationship with this guy could work out. But it is probably not a good idea to expect this one to be the guy with whom you tie the knot, raise the kid, or grow old gracefully.

Helpful Hints
Important questions to ask yourself:

1. Does he respect your wishes when you ask him not to look at other women? When you are out together, is he able to focus solely on you?
2. Is he someone you can just play with and not get hurt?
3. What are your expectations for the relationship, and have you checked with him or seen any evidence to suggest he shares them?

Things to Do

Find out if he has ever been involved in a long-term adult relationship. This is also definitely the kind of guy to get to know over time before you leap into living together or any other long-term commitments. Give it a shot if you believe he is a keeper, but if you find yourself feeling rejected by his diminishing attention, always remember, fresh opportunities exist for you as well.

13. Fan or Fanatic

Personality

It's easy to admire a man who works to make the world a better place. Whether the source of his passion is politics, religion, the environment, social justice, or living a green lifestyle, this is a guy with ideals and commitment.

All of those things are admirable qualities. My only word of caution is that there is a world of difference between a *Fan* and a *Fanatic*. A *Fan* feels passion and enthusiasm for whatever issue or cause is important to him, while a *Fanatic* is someone who is arrogant and rigid about his beliefs.

The *Fan* inspires, whereas the *Fanatic* condemns.

My friend Ellen dated a guy, Dean, who was sweet, caring, and attentive. He had excellent values and morals, and Ellen was crazy about him. Dean was Christian, and Ellen, who was raised Catholic, loved the similarities of their religious backgrounds.

The relationship had been going very well for two months, when Ellen invited Dean to a birthday celebration with her most intimate friends. Dean was welcomed, and his charm and wit won over Ellen's friends.

Toward the end of the evening, one of Ellen's girlfriends mentioned that the next morning she was going to attend a chant session. She was a Buddhist, and chanting was a regular practice for her and her husband. Dean piped up calmly but with fervor, "Have you ever checked out the Bible?" She answered, "Yes," and that sparked some interesting banter about holy books and religion. At this point, Ellen felt fine. Dean had simply expressed his point of view. But when Dean then added, "Our Lord Jesus Christ is the true way, you know," Ellen froze. The evening ended shortly after that comment, and, on the way home, Dean pontificated about who would go to heaven and who would not. Ellen felt disenchanted and broke it off. She could love a man who held strong religious beliefs, but she could not love a man who was so strident and closed-minded that he divided the world into the saved and the damned.

A *Fanatic* needs to confirm his view again and again. He lacks a healthy respect for different points of view or choices. His causes or beliefs distort how he looks at everything else in his life. He lacks flexibility and tolerance.

This could be just as true of an environmentalist as a Bible thumper. It's admirable to see a guy live his beliefs, and in the case of the environmentalist, recycle rather than waste or purchase a Prius instead of a Hummer. But if the mere sight of a Hummer or of someone failing to recycle sends him into a self-righteous fit, then you may want to think twice.

Attractiveness

Our lives can be enriched by men who care deeply about things other than themselves. A vegetarian might influence you to eat better, a conservationist might help you to discover the outdoors, a political activist might spur you to become more involved in your community. It's great when a partner broadens our world.

It speaks well of a man's character if he gives money, his time, or talent to a cause or his faith. This kind of guy has far more appeal than one who is apathetic or cynical. At best, his values may reflect a desire to make the world a better place, and at some point this might include your own family and children. It's only when a *Fan* becomes a *Fanatic* that this type of guy becomes a problem.

Challenges

I was at a party recently where a thirty-something guy was talking to a group of us about the curse of our dependence on foreign oil. He couldn't understand why everyone didn't rush out to buy a Prius. I admired his passion and agreed with a lot of what he said. I remember the 1960s and what it felt like to have such passion. But then this guy called the American public "stupid and complacent." All of us flinched at this accusation. After all, weren't we part of the American public? We took it personally. This is the challenge with the *Fanatic*; he can't stop himself from climbing atop his soapbox and preaching.

The *Fanatic* can't allow anyone else to hold a different opinion. In some cases, he's so consumed by his cause or mission that the relationship takes a backseat. In other situations, this guy's view of life is so distorted by this one issue that he loses all sense of balance and perspective.

For instance, let's say you're celebrating Christmas with your family, and your partner happens to be a vegetarian. A *Fan* eats his soy ham and tofu turkey and stuffing and thanks your mother for thoughtfully providing a vegetarian dish for him. The *Fanatic*, on the other hand, isn't content to simply eat his veggie dinner. Instead, he has to spoil everyone else's dinner by making a crack about eating defenseless animals.

In short, the *Fan* is a guy who lives by his convictions. The *Fanatic* requires a foe and insists on policing other people's behavior.

Helpful Hints
Important questions to ask yourself:

1. Do his beliefs distort the way he looks at the entire world? Is this comfortable for you?
2. Is he passionate and enthusiastic, or arrogant and rigid? Is this embarrassing for you?
3. Does his orthodoxy or certainty require you to live by his rules? Does he condemn or belittle you, your family, or friends who disagree with him?

Things to Do

It's easy to support the *Fan*. Sure, he may get carried away by his passions, but a healthy bit of teasing or a difference of opinion can add spice to a relationship. With a *Fan*, you don't have to adopt his convictions. A healthy man should appreciate your point of view. You can both agree to disagree.

If your guy is a *Fanatic*, you might consider jumping on his bandwagon. If you believe in the cause, and he is willing to monitor his fervor to a more manageable degree, this could be something you share and do together. You can set boundaries by insisting that he respect yours and others' opinions. A toned-downed *Fanatic* might add excitement to your life.

If joining his cause isn't your cup of tea, you may have to be patient and low-key to offset his need to convince everyone of the truth of his beliefs. If he meets all of your other needs, perhaps you can reach a healthy balance with a *Fanatic*.

If he is obnoxious and arrogant and obsessed with his personal truth, or patronizes you and views you and everyone else as less enlightened, then he is a poor choice. Find salvation, and show him the door.

14. Mr. Lives in Pictures

Personality

This man has a movie theater inside his head. He is a walking, breathing Cineplex. In his mind, he directs and stars in film after film, each of them worthy of an Academy Award. He's always the hero, and each story is romantic, adventurous, and has a happy ending. The content of his script changes depending on his immediate environment. When with a woman, he invents the perfect fantasy romance. When on a new job, he imagines his meteoric rise to the top of the firm. In his mental film fantasy, everything works out great with everyone fulfilled. What eventually happens is that real life seldom lives up to his fantasy, and the script of what he desires keeps changing.

A female client, Lynn came to one of my seminars for some career guidance. She had a healthy sense of self and appeared to be very happy in her one-and-a-half-year relationship with Steve. Their plans were to work in Los Angeles for one or two more years and then move to Oregon, where they planned to buy land, build a house, and raise animals and a couple of kids. I remember telling Lynn, "How beautiful! What a great life that will be."

We mapped out a plan and she left happy. But after several months, she came back with Steve, to address his lack of a focused career plan.

Lynn complained that their problem started when she was talking with one of Steve's best friends, an actor, who told her, "I think that Steve has a good shot at a successful acting career." The friend added, "I want to help him in any way I can." Shocked by this statement, Lynn asked, "What acting career?"

She approached Steve, who confided that when he hangs out with his actor friends, he's reminded of how he's always wanted to act. So, he decided, why not get some 8 × 10 photos printed and give it a shot? Lynn asked him how this fit in with running an organic garden and starting a family together in Oregon.

I listened as the two of them revisited the topic in my office.

Steve: "Oh, I want to do that, too! I think we could have beautiful kids together. I can already see them running through the yard, our vegetable garden, our whole happy, healthy family."

Lynn: "How can you get an acting career going while working to save money for our move? And how can you leave L.A. if you are going to be an actor?"

Steve sat there with a defensive look on his face. In his head, it all made perfect sense. With his buddies, he imagined himself acting in indie films. When he was with Lynn, he saw himself playing the role of mountain man, *selling organic boutique produce to gourmet restaurants in Portland.* It became clear that Steve held still more scenarios of how his life might yet play out.

When hanging out with his single guy friends, he checked out other women and lapsed into a "I'm a single guy in L.A. checking out the babes," mind-set, though it was clear he had no intention of cheating on Lynn.

When visiting his mother, with whom he was very close, Steve played the title role in, *Don't Worry Mom, I'll always be There for You."*

It became clear that Steve harbored untold versions of how he imagined his life might yet unfold. After a lunch with some of his more entrepreneurial buddies, Steve became keen to make millions with a multilevel marketing franchise selling Ginkgo biloba energy drinks and vitamins made from Goji berries. He even fantasized about the free trip he would receive by being the highest seller in the company.

Fantasy and imagining can play a positive role in anyone's life, but for *Mr. Lives in Pictures*, his mind is like a multiplex theatre, and on any given day a new film fantasy of his life plays out at 3:00 PM, 5:30 PM, 8:00 PM and 10:15 PM. The plot is contingent on his mood and environment. The problem isn't that a guy weighs or imagines a range of occupations or approaches to life with a high degree of openness and sense of possibility. This mind-set, when backed with focus and perseverance, can produce extremely successful self-made men. The key difference with *Mr. Lives in Pictures* is that there is little chance of him actually following through on a single scenario, let alone him reinventing his life over and over again with each new plot twist he edits into the script.

What Lynn came to realize is that Steve's vision of a home and buying land in Oregon had no more chance of coming to fruition than his acting career, multilevel marketing scheme, or untold other dreams. Steve hadn't consciously lied to Lynn. The fantasy of a life with her, kids, and a rustic home in rural Oregon truly appealed to him. In his mental fantasyland, there was plenty of time for him to be an actor and then an organic farmer and father and entrepreneur, and he simply didn't understand why Lynn was so upset.

For her part, Lynn began to realize that raising a family and the Oregon farm might never happen. Steve's reality shifted too often to gauge what a life with him might hold. Although heartbroken, Lynn moved on and has since gotten married to a stockbroker and is living in the hills of Los Angeles with a beautiful baby daughter. The last she heard from Steve, he was thinking of going back to school to pursue a graduate degree.

All of us have a narrative of one kind or another playing in our heads. The trouble with *Mr. Lives in Pictures* is that the source of pleasure from his fantasy of what might be is more powerful than reality.

Attractiveness

These men can create a beautiful picture of how your life together can unfold. What woman doesn't yearn for that perfect person who can imagine the same beautiful future together as she does. *Mr. Lives in Pictures* is one of the most seductive of all the male types, and one of the most innocent and naive. If you are not attached to your future turning out a specific way, and he is able to pull his weight in supporting the relationship, life with this type of guy can work for you.

After all, these guys are often passionate, creative, and excited about life. They certainly are not lazy, they are seldom bored, and they can make for interesting company. Mostly, these men are not malicious, they are just dreamers. They truly believe it is all possible and that there's plenty of time to do everything they want. If you share this outlook and are also a bit of a free spirit, life with this guy can be enchanting!

Mr. Lives in Pictures might fantasize that he will be a famous actor, a six-figure-a-year earner or world-renowned writer, but it doesn't necessarily mean he plans to leave you to do it. *Mr. Lives in Pictures* is perfectly capable of being a faithful partner. Fantasy is fulfillment enough for him, and he might love that you are by his side on his many journeys.

Challenges

Mr. Lives in Pictures is really only for women for whom consistent stability and security are not important. For everyone else, he will be frustrating. His giddiness for new possibilities can grow tiring, and you may soon find yourself thinking, "He paints a beautiful picture of our future together, but I wonder if he can pull any of it off." Stability and success are unlikely for him, although by trying many careers, sometimes simultaneously, he might eke out a living, albeit a meager one. I have actually seen a few *Mr. Lives in Pictures* become very successful. What they lack in preparation they sometimes make up for with enthusiasm or by being at the right place at the right time.

Perhaps it is their fear of boredom that keeps them scripting new movies, or a fear of failure that keeps them from ever finding out what they're really made of. Whatever the reason, *Mr. Lives in Pictures* is a risky ticket.

Helpful Hints
Important questions to ask yourself:

1. If you think your guy is in this category, ask him, "What do you see yourself doing one year from now, three years from now, or in ten to twenty years?" How do you feel about his answers?

2. Is he willing to work with you on creating a plan that allows for his need for possibility and reinvention, but also your need for stability? Is he able to honor some sort of compromise?

3. Is a relationship with a guy who's always excited about the next thing appealing enough to outweigh a lack of stability or certainty?

4. Is your guy one of the *Mr. Lives in Pictures* who is able to be faithful, or does he require a new leading lady for each new film?

Things to Do

We all have dreams and aspirations. Perhaps the two of you could create a storyboard—the sequence of drawings used to plot movies—as a way of mapping out your life together. Cover a large board with the images of the home, children, or other elements of the life you hope to share together over the coming months and years. You could call this film *Our Life of Love, Adventure, and Passion.*

Think of it as a vision board, and one that can help you and your partner create a sense of direction. And if he wishes to change course, or add a new scene, then the two of you can discuss how it will contribute or take away from the story of your life together.

If he is able to maintain commitments and meet you at least halfway, you might have a keeper. Although a relationship with *Mr. Lives in Pictures* will never be predictable, you might come to find his creativity inspiring. It certainly won't be boring!

15. Bullies

Personality

Bullies are people who get their jollies from intimidating others. Not all *Bullies* are violent, although many have this tendency. What all *Bullies* share is a need to verbally, psychologically, or physically dominate someone whom they perceive to be weaker than themselves.

I remember when I was eight years old, there was this boy we all used to play with after school on the playground across the street from my house. He was about eleven, and he would make all the girls take off their shoes and walk on jagged stones. We were afraid of him and did as he ordered, never telling anyone of his actions. In hindsight, I imagine he was abused at home and took it out on us. But whatever his story, I suspect that today he is in a relationship and making some woman miserable.

Bullies, like many of the types described in this book, have brittle self-esteem. They defy stereotypes. They might be rich and educated or poor and high school dropouts. A *Bully's* agenda is to intimidate, control, and manipulate in order to feel better about himself. Dominating others gives him a sense of power and control. The most insidious part is the *Bully* often has the ability to convince you that if he hits you, psychologically or physically, it is your fault and that you deserve it.

Another type of *Bully* is not as overt as the type who uses his fists. This *Bully* is crafty, manipulative, and scheming, and has a shrewd ability to belittle and demean. This guy assesses his victim's vulnerabilities and slowly, through a twisted kind of verbal water torture, wears her down. Without even raising a hand, he pummels his victim into submission.

I did some Stress and Anger Management sessions with a couple whose names were Jason and Ali. A handsome couple in their mid-thirties, he was a wealthy investment banker and she a successful model. In short, they were a hip L.A. couple, with a Mercedes, beautiful home, and a chic lifestyle.

Ali came to see me first. She told me that Jason was a great guy, but that they fought a lot. She wanted it to work, but she was confused about what to do. He wanted to get married in a few months, but she was feeling reticent.

The next session, they came in together. I asked them what they wanted to talk about. I still recall much of that conversation:

Jason: "Allison is a great gal and I love her, but I feel that she has low self-esteem, and I want her to know how great she is."

I asked Ali if this was true for her.

Ali: "I don't know. I used to think I felt good about myself, but I feel confused a lot now. Sometimes I feel…"

Jason interrupted: "See what I mean? She has everything going for her, but talking to her is a waste of time. She never believes what I tell her. Ali, why are you like that? What's wrong with you?"

Ali: "I don't know. I …"

Jason interrupted again: "Like the other night at the dinner party, you never spoke up and joined the conversation. It's common sense to engage in conversation at a party. Everyone was talking and laughing, and you were silent. If you loved me, you wouldn't embarrass me like that!"

Ali: "You make me feel afraid to speak sometimes."

Jason: "Ali, I make you feel afraid? So it's my fault? I don't make you feel that. It's your issue, and if you continue to blame me for your low self-esteem, we can never get any better. Right, Doc?"

Now the attention was on me. I calmly asked Jason, "What do you need from Ali that you are not getting?"

Jason: "I want her to love herself and act right."

Me: "For whom?"

Jason: For herself! That's a crazy question. Don't you get it? Here I've laid the entire problem out and you can't even see it?"

Me: "I do see some problems here, and I am seeing it's not all one-sided."

Jason: "Well, I can tell talking to you will be a waste of time. I've come here to help my lady be healthier, and, because you're a woman, all you can do is shake your 'bad boy' finger at me!"

Within a few minutes, Jason had displayed an array of bullying tactics. He did his best to intimidate, embarrass, and confuse Ali, and he did so without so much as raising his voice.

When he tried to tangle me up in his ploy, my unwillingness to be bullied caused him to leave the session early, and Ali and I talked about what had happened. She realized that Jason found fault with most women and she decided to break it off. And interestingly enough, a few weeks later she sent me an email saying she felt great.

Attractiveness

Similar to *The Loose Cannon,* these guys can be great mates until this tendency surfaces, and you realize that you are being mistreated. Classic *Bullies* tend to be more transparent and easier to recognize. The more scheming *Bullies* are crafty, and they know how to woo as well as to belittle. Some of these men are smart enough to put on a public face to everyone else in your life, so that you're constantly told how lucky you are to be with such an attentive and wonderful guy. I've known men who hit their wives in the morning, then showered their mothers or sisters with compliments and kindness that afternoon.

Just like *The Salesman,* this guy knows how to make it look as if he has put your needs first. If you fall for his tactics, don't blame yourself, he's good.

Challenges

There's no mincing of words: *Bullies* are mean-spirited and nasty. Their personality as tormenters developed early in life, and they are unlikely to change. A major hurdle is that bullying works, and *Bullies* know this. Unless there's an overwhelming desire on his part to change, coupled with therapy, your life with a *Bully* will be confusing, demeaning, and torturous. And the more sensitive, fair, and empathic you are, the more you can be bamboozled by his manipulative skills.

Helpful Hints
Important questions to ask yourself:

1. Does your guy insult you with belittling comments, make unreasonable demands, yell, glare, or intimidate you on a regular basis? Do you feel it's your fault that he does this?
2. Does he use mind games or other manipulative tactics to try to confuse, intimidate, or control you?
3. Does he blame, threaten, or discount you when you make attempts to make things better?
4. Has he ever been physically violent with you? Are you or your family afraid of what destructive thing he might do next?

Things to Do

The best thing to do with *Bullies* is to avoid them. Learn to be aware of bullying tactics by recognizing narcissistic, self-centered, or passive-aggressive behaviors.

If you are with a *Bully*, you must let him know that his bullying days are over. He is no longer allowed to put you down, and you are no longer allowed to believe his negative view of you.

And if he has you frightened for your safety, please seek help from the authorities or groups that provide services and shelter for women fleeing domestic violence. Although a *Bully* is often the product of an abusive childhood, you need not also become a victim of his past.

16. Glory Days Guy

Personality

In the 1990's sitcom *Married with Children*, the main character, Al, is a wisecracking, beer-drinking, blue-collar, politically incorrect shoe salesman who is certain his freedom vanished the day he got married. As he sees it, Peg, who he married right out of high school, and his two smart-ass teenagers, have robbed all joy from his life, except for the pleasure he takes in arguing with them.

Yet Al does not see himself as a total loser. Oh, no! In high school he scored four touchdowns in a single game. He had been a football hero, and he relives that glorious moment over and over again.

This is a *Glory Days Guy*, who in high school, college, the service, or in some other situation way back when was triumphant. The problem is, he has done little since then, and he must rely on his memories of his glory days to feel good about himself.

There's nothing wrong with having achieved something in one's past. The question is what prevents this guy from creating an inspired future? Maybe this guy had some hard knocks and lost his footing for a while. He might secretly yearn for a better life. We can all understand the desire to accomplish great things and improve our lives, but some of these guys aren't willing or able to do the work to get there.

Some of these guys manage to find a modicum of peace from their past accomplishments. I once had a neighbor, Frank, who was in his sixties, single, with a modest job at a warehouse. He rented a room in the house across the street. He had attended Woodstock and had fulfilled many of his dreams and fantasies back in the sixties. Frank, who seemed to enjoy life, loved to reminisce about those giddy days with his buddies and his girlfriend, who adored him. This kind of *Glory Days Guy* is not going to be a problem, as many other types of these men can be. As long as you feel inspired about your life together, this guy can be a fine partner.

Attractiveness

These guys have great stories, are proud of what they've done, and are usually jovial, until they've had a few too many drinks. Then the melancholy side comes out. Some of these guys are just the opposite. Those men are melancholy until they've had a few drinks, and that's when their jovial side emerges. Either way, these men, at the right moment or in the right company, can be a lot of fun and often carry a certain charisma. They know that they once achieved greatness and are proud of it. It's easy to feel tender toward these men as they seek to rekindle those days when they felt good about themselves and what they were able to accomplish.

Challenges

If he is not the Frank type of *Glory Days Guy*, unless this guy is able to figure out a way to enrich his life in the present, he can end up clinically depressed or end up turning to drugs or alcohol. The glory of the past will wear thin as he ages and will serve as a reminder in a negative sense as to how far he's fallen. The point is, this guy needs something in his life now to get excited about. If not, buddies will move on, and people will tire of his stories. If you are with him at this time, you might end up feeling burdened with having become his sole source of emotional support.

Helpful Hints
Important questions to ask yourself:

1. Is your *Glory Days Guy* afraid to move forward in his life? Is he hiding in the past to cover a lack of motivation, clarity, or direction?
2. Is he often depressed, and does he abuse drugs or alcohol?
3. Can you live with someone who might not have a new set of stories?

Things to Do

If he relishes the past so much that he is unaware of the present, suggest hobbies or other pursuits at which he can excel. If he has rhythm, suggest dance lessons; if he's coordinated, try golf; if he's handy, plan a project in the home. Try to get him involved in anything that will allow him to feel good about himself and help him to recognize his gifts and talents. Often, a *Glory Days Guy* doesn't like his job, so something outside of work can stoke winning feelings and provide him with new stories. This guy doesn't know that he is enough. Anything you can do to help him see that he is enough will comfort him.

If he can balance his past and his present, he can be a keeper. But if you sense an underlying, intractable misery at the heart of his persona, you might want to leave this guy in your past.

17. The Sensitive Male

Personality

There are many masculine men who are sensitive. Indeed, it's my experience that most men are far more sensitive than they appear to be, and as a woman, I appreciate and respect this quality.

The Sensitive Male I am referring to here is the guy whose female side is more developed than his maleness.

Let me make it clear up front that I am not talking about the male-dominant, traditional gender roles depicted in fifties sitcoms. Quite the contrary, I fully support equality between the sexes, and my intention isn't to delineate how women or men should behave within strictly defined roles.

What I am referring to are *energies*, aspects of maleness and femaleness. In my experience, a relationship needs a balance of both. Typically, to achieve this harmony, one partner expresses a more masculine energy—logical, assertive, dominant, and left-brained, and the other a more feminine energy—intuitive, receptive, nurturing, and right-brained. I've found this to be as true in gay relationships as in heterosexual unions. Defined thousands of years ago in ancient Chinese texts, a yin and yang balance is necessary and natural in any partnership.

In most cultures, men have adopted what we have come to think of as male energy, and to some degree, most women exude a female energy. For most men, there is a primary need to be respected, and women feel a need to be protected. This balanced combination, this yin and yang, allows each person to exude his or her dominant nature, creating a sense of a natural or organic fit to the relationship. If, for example, a woman's male side is more dominant than her feminine side, *The Sensitive Male* can work out for her.

This is not to say that any of us are always one way all the time. According to Carl Jung, every man has a feminine, intuitive side, and every woman possesses a masculine, rational side. In the course of a relationship, partners adopt certain roles, such as who does what chores.

It seems that many of the problems couples have can be traced to a confusion and/or imbalance in masculine-feminine balance.

This type of guy, *The Sensitive Male*, is the man who values his ability to feel deeply more than his ability to take control. His reactions might be more emotional than logical, which might leave his partner feeling as if she doesn't have a rock to lean on. The character of Niles Crane from the TV show *Frasier*, exemplifies this type of man, as does the character Allan from *Two and a Half Men*.

Tina, a doctor who took my Movement Expression Therapy class, was married to Stuart, also a well-respected physician. Stuart was a sweet, loving man who had a great rapport with his patients. Tina loved him and had initially been attracted to him after dating a man who was cold, distant, and emotionally unavailable. Stuart was very much emotionally available, and the couple would chat for hours about their innermost feelings. This became a key aspect of their relationship, and Stuart freely shared his emotions with Tina. At the same time, he also began yielding some of his household duties to Tina. These ranged from fixing things around the house to keeping up maintenance on their cars. When a problem arose with a contractor who had tried to bilk them for shoddy construction work done in their kitchen, it fell to Tina to fight it out with the contractor. Stuart shied away from confrontations with other men.

At the end of one of the classes, Tina confided, "What I loved about Stuart at first is now causing me to be upset with him. I want to be the woman and for him to be the guy. Now I find our roles reversed, or at best confusing."

What clinched it for her was during a big earthquake, when Stuart panicked, and she had to hunt for a flashlight and calm his nerves. Not too many months later, they divorced.

Tina and Stuart might have worked because Stuart was a great guy, a skilled doctor, an excellent provider, and conscientious partner who loved Tina. He even did some thoughtful little things, such as bringing her tea every morning. But Tina wanted to express herself within a primary feminine role and for Stuart to fill a more traditional masculine role. When they couldn't find a compromise, they split up.

Stuart is remarried to a wonderful attorney with a highly developed male side who loves Stuart's sensitivity and caring. Stuart feels loved for being exactly who he is.

Tina married a computer programmer with a strong sense of masculinity, and she relishes being the one who brings a feminine energy to the relationship.

Attractiveness

These sensitive guys are good listeners, understand a woman's need to express her feelings, and are typically attentive and empathetic partners. They can be great stay-at-home dads and are often gifted in their interactions with children and pets. Unlike many men, they tend to freely share domestic tasks, such as cooking or changing diapers. Women who chafe at always having to take care of the home can find *Sensitive Males* very attractive. If you are a more take-charge, assertive woman who wishes to be out –in–the world making your mark, *The Sensitive Male* might be exactly what you need.

Challenges

The main challenge with *The Sensitive Male* is to be very clear if you need him to assume a more masculine-dominant role. If it is important for you to express your feminine side in most circumstances, this guy is not for you.

If you have been toying with the idea that this could work for you—and these really can be wonderful men in so many ways—here's a word of caution. Beware of *Sensitive Males* who are essentially weak. There is a big difference between a man who is receptive and nurturing, and a partner who is weak or passive. Do not partner with a *Sensitive Male* who fears the world, finds it overwhelming, or retreats from all conflict. If your guy is powerless in the face of life's curve balls, you will end up being his mother, nurse, provider, support system, and therapist. A timid and passive *Sensitive Male* will exhaust you.

Although *The Sensitive Male* has many great qualities, he will never be a strong alpha, masculine, George Clooney, Christian Bale kind of guy. If you have a strong need to be with a take-charge, rock-solid kind of guy, this type of man is probably not for you.

Helpful Hints
Important questions to ask yourself:

1. Do you feel that both your feminine and masculine sides are well developed? If you had to pick one as being the one you would prefer to be more dominant in a relationship, which would it be?
2. Is your guy's masculine quotient to your liking? Where is he lacking? Where is he strong?
3. Do you respect him? Does he take care of you in the way that you like to be taken care of?
4. Are you male dominant to the extent that he might feel his own masculinity is eclipsed? Is this causing problems in the relationship?

Things to Do

The Sensitive Male's receptivity can work to your advantage. Talk to him if you feel you need him to be more assertive. *Sensitive Males* are great listeners. It can be difficult for your guy to stretch and rise to the occasion if you are taking care of everything, so offer clear guidance so he can step up to the plate. Whenever he does a traditional masculine task, let him know that it makes you feel safe, happy, and taken care of. These men often feel better about themselves when they tap into their masculine selves, so encourage it, praise it, and be appreciative.

Perhaps the two of you can strike a healthy balance. With care and a little work, your *Sensitive Male* might be the man of your dreams. They're not for everyone, but these guys can be great catches.

18. Substance Abuser

Personality

Let's be honest, most of us seek some form of escape from the pressures and realities of life. My own indulgences tend toward a glass of wine, a hot bath, or a good comedy show.

However, if you're dating a man who copes with life's stresses with excessive drinking, a daily joint, or a line of coke to face work, this is a huge red flag. With some drugs, such as crystal meth, crack, or heroin, even occasional use is a major cause for concern. Even some legal meds, such as Vicodin, Valium, or OxyContin, can be abused and might be a sign that your guy is not in a position to maintain a stable relationship.

Of course, I'm not talking about a guy who enjoys a glass or two of wine with dinner, a beer or two after work, or a social drink. Your partner has a substance abuse problem if he habitually indulges to excess, obsesses about it, plans for it, and most importantly, his personality changes if he doesn't get it.

Addiction stems from deep, unresolved psychological issues. Even a great guy with many wonderful qualities who abuses drugs or alcohol and won't seek treatment is unlikely to work out. Growing up, I witnessed firsthand the havoc of living with an alcoholic at home. That past, along with my own bad relationship choices and observing my friends and clients, has shown me that, simply put, a person who is not a *Substance Abuser* cannot live happily with a person who is. Bottom line: your priorities are too different. The user's priority is his fix, hit, drink, or smoke, and that takes precedence over everything else, including you, children, and his job.

Attractiveness

If you are attracted to an addict, it's for one of three reasons: (1) you share the same or a similar addiction, (2) you are aware that he uses some, but are unaware of how big the problem is, or you do know about the problem but are choosing denial, or (3) you have no idea that there is a problem.

If the attraction is because of the first reason, then you need help, too. Addiction is a disease and requires professional intervention.

If the attraction is because of the second or third reason, it tells me that you really like this guy. Addicts are people. They come in all shapes, sizes, and personalities. Yours might be funny, talented, or charming. The part of his personality you're failing to consider is his addiction. Unless your partner recognizes his addiction, seeks and follows through with treatment, your love for him alone is not enough. All of his great qualities will mean little as his addiction becomes the focal point of the relationship.

Challenges

This guy will have a hard time showing up for you in life—emotionally, psychologically, or physically. He will not allow anything to get in the way of his need. There's the classic story of daddy (or mommy) not making it to the kid's recital, because he (or she) is getting drunk. I've heard this story more times than I can count.

The addict is inherently narcissistic. He will put his need for his substance above all else, even if it is destroying him. That raises another challenge—when his health starts to fail, do you want to spend your life taking care of a sick addict?

Helpful Hints
Important questions to ask yourself:

1. What are his vices? Is he being truthful? Do you see any changes in his personality that you don't understand?
2. Are you OK with what you've come to accept in regard to his drinking or substance use?
3. If you have established that he has a problem, is he aware that he does? Is he getting help?

Things to Do

First off, here's what not to do: Do not make the mistake of assuming your love is enough to rehabilitate him. Only professionals can help him. Period.

Unless he enters a twelve-step program, rehab, or therapy that addresses his problem and he commits and sticks to it, it's best to simply get out. My own relationship experience has shown me that being with someone who is struggling with an addiction is a miserable experience. Life with an addict who will not seek help never has a happy ending. You can't fix someone who won't take responsibility for helping himself. Run.

Note: The above holds true for most any addiction, including men who are sexaholics. A sexaholic is someone who has an extensive porn collection, visits porn sites daily, frequents strip clubs, and visits prostitutes. The Internet rankles many women because it makes pornography readily available to husbands and boyfriends. But just as we distinguished between a person who drinks in moderation from the alcoholic, the same is true of a man who might enjoy viewing porn and one whose life is defined by it.

19. He's a Young Thing and Cannot Leave His Mother

Personality

Whether this guy lives at home with Mom or not is irrelevant. Because whether or not he lives down the hall or across the country, he is too close to her, and she is too involved in his life. Regardless of his age, he's still Momma's good little boy. No matter how hard you try, you're still not going to live up to Mom's standards.

There's nothing rational about it, except from *Young Thing's* psychological point of view. Momma cherished him as a boy, and for him to place any other woman above her risks losing her doting attention.

Men with such deep attachments to their mothers can exhibit a wide range of behaviors. At one end of the spectrum is *The Young Thing* who has his own life, friends, a good job, and is capable of a relationship. He'll have a girlfriend or might even be married with kids. But Mom, even if she's in Miami and he's in Malibu, sits (metaphorically speaking) on his shoulder, whispering in his ear, influencing most of his choices. He might not be aware that she's there, and he might even profess a wish to get rid of her, but Momma's needs and expectations are so entrenched in his psyche that they're not easily removed. His mom might even be a far cry from the television sitcom stereotype of the meddling Jewish or Italian mother. Her influence can be subtle, but it is not easily ignored.

One of my Anger Management clients, George came in with his fiancée, Mindy for some coaching and to address some anger issues arising around the planning of their wedding. Mindy loved George but felt he was too influenced by his mother's opinions. George disagreed and said he was just trying to keep the peace.

"She just wants to help," George said. "She's always been very helpful with my projects."

"Your projects?" Mindy said, "This is our wedding! She's too pushy! She's always telling you what to do. She hates my dress and the caterer I picked! She is trying to control everything!"

George fell silent. He could not dispute Mindy's assessment. He knew it was true, and he looked defeated, as if tugged in two directions.

I asked him, "George, how often do you hear your mother's voice in your head, commenting on your daily activities?"

He paused, and after a few moments, replied, "Oh, my God, she talks to me all day. She comments on just about everything I do. I'm not just talking about on the phone, I hear her in my head!"

I then asked, "How long has this been happening? What age did it start?"

George thought a moment and replied, "Well, when I first moved away to college, she would call me every day to check in on me. None of the other guys had their mothers calling every day. It was embarrassing. She's always been too involved in my life and too controlling. When I told her she could only call twice a week, she cried and was upset, saying I was being insensitive and hurtful. Even though I began screening her calls, she still remains in my thoughts, telling me what to do."

"Do you feel guilty that you asked her to only call twice a week?" I continued.

"Yes, I do. I remember I felt bad, like a bad son." He paused, "But I am not a bad son!"

"Are you ready to let go of the guilt and focus your attention 100 percent on your fiancée and upcoming wedding?" I asked.

George said yes and was clearly relieved. It was as if he had been waiting fifteen years for someone to give him permission to not feel the guilt his mother inflicted on him anymore.

From that moment on, George began setting new boundaries, and he strove to put Mindy first. He hadn't realized that his situation was worse than if his mom had moved into a spare room, because he had allowed her to take up permanent residence in his head.

Mindy reported back to me a few months later that the wedding had been fantastic, and that George, by setting boundaries, had shifted the dynamic with his mother. His mother had become less intrusive and demanding of him.

A smart mother will be flexible and adjust. She won't want to lose her son, though it is up to the son to be firm with her.

At the other end of the spectrum is *The Young Thing* who will not, under any circumstances, sever the cord between him and his mother.

He will not only put her first, but he will even compare you to her. She probably won't like you or any of his ex-girlfriends. No one is good enough for her boy. At best, she'll tolerate you. These guys are psychologically stuck around age six or seven, an age when Mom is still the most important person in his world.

One of my friends, Sydney, was dating a man named Martin. They were getting serious and had started talking about moving in together. Sydney told me that the only concern she had about the relationship was the intensity of Martin's closeness with his mother, Ann. Mother and son spoke every day, giggling on the phone. When Sydney and Martin went out to dinner, his mother often joined them, sitting at his side. They even nibbled food off of each other's plates.

Sydney found this odd and approached Martin about it. He said to her, "You don't understand, because you don't have a close relationship with your mother."

One day, Ann chastised Sydney, saying, "I don't think you are cooking the right foods for my Martin. He has a sensitive stomach." Martin replied, "Thanks, Mom, you always take such good care of me." Sydney was furious, and she decided to hold off on moving in with Martin.

The following week, Sydney told me that when she and Martin and his extended family were leaving a restaurant, Ann literally jumped on Martin's back and rode piggyback through the parking lot, giggling. None of the rest of the family said anything or seemed to find this behavior odd.

Sydney was shocked. In one way or another, she realized, Martin would carry his mother along with him wherever they went. She decided to end the relationship.

Attractiveness

These guys tend to be sweet and fun to be around. They are playful and are used to doting on woman, and this can feel really nice. They received so much attention from their mothers as children that they feel cherished, and as a result they have often achieved a fair amount of success.

Some also might have family money and are able to afford a great home and the means to travel.

Challenges

Mindy and George's situation shows that many of these guys are able to find a healthy balance between Mom and you. The challenge is for you to be clear, calm, and firm in expressing your needs. You will have to avoid getting too emotional, or your guy will just be immobilized. Two emotional, needy women will be too much for him to handle, so it's best to approach this subject with calm.

But with guys like Martin, the challenge of weaning them from their addiction to Momma's love and approval will be far tougher. If you find him unable and unwilling to change this dynamic, or he is unconscious that there is even an issue, you might find it best to move on.

Helpful Hints
Important questions to ask yourself:

1. Does your guy spend too much time with his mom? Does he often talk about her and refer to her? Is there a dependency between them that feels excessive?
2. Does she interfere with your lives in ways you find detrimental? Does she try to control you?
3. Does he compare you to her? Does she put you down?

Things to Do

As mentioned in the section on Challenges, the George type might be workable. Make clear requests of him: "The next time we go out with your mother, can you please be warm to me and let her see that I'm important to you, too? Can you include me so I don't feel shut out?" or "If your mother says anything critical to me, I want you to tell her it's unacceptable and stand up for me." If he starts to defend her, stay calm and say, "I understand you have a close relationship with your mother, but I'm important, too. We will have to find a compromise." Hopefully, over time, he will hear you.

If she criticizes you, tell her that it is not OK for her to do that. In *A Cure for the Common Life,* I say, "No one is so important that they have the right to mistreat or abuse you."

But if your guy prefers Momma's apron strings to you, you might want to reexamine why you're with him, and what you're getting out of the relationship. If the situation doesn't improve, you might decide it's best to bid both mother and boyfriend adieu.

20. Mr. Know-It-All

Personality

I once spotted a handwritten flier pinned to a notice board with the words:

FOR SALE
Encyclopedia Britannica, complete set.
Like new, hardly used. Don't need it.
Friggin' husband knows everything!

Although I gather it was penned by someone with a good sense of humor, it happens to be a perfect description of *Mr. Know-It-All*. Indeed, this guy is convinced he knows everything. He's sure he is never wrong. He will discuss, argue, and rant about religion, art, business, medicine, politics, the Yankees, the stock market, biodynamic gardening, Civil War history, and any other topic you might mention. No matter the subject, he believes himself to be an expert.

How did he come to acquire his supposed wisdom? It varies. Some *Mr. Know-It-Alls* graduated from Ivy League schools or earned advanced degrees. These men feel they have proof that they know it all. Others might rule the roost at work or might have made money in financial fields or real estate markets, so in their minds, their financial success is their credential. Still others read a lot of arcane journals or books that they feel have bestowed upon them a rarefied degree of knowledge.

It is hard to tell which type is the most intolerable. On the opposite end of the spectrum of the overachiever, *Mr. Know-It-All* is the guy with no more than a high-school education, limited professional success, who never cracks a book, yet somehow thinks himself smarter than everyone else around him. These self-proclaimed Einsteins are the kind of men who attract and lord over women with poor self-esteem.

But all of these *Know-It-Alls* share one thing in common. Regardless of their real or imagined wisdom, they have an overwhelming need to be right. Should you make the mistake of questioning their expertise, you are fishing for an argument.

Several friends and I were out one evening. We had gone to the theatre and were enjoying a late-night snack at a restaurant. My friend, Kate, had come with her new boyfriend, Gary, who seemed nice enough. After talking a bit about the

Stephen Sondheim musical we'd just seen, we asked Gary to share his thoughts.

He proceeded to explain why our interpretation of a particular lyric was dead wrong and then illuminated us as to "what it really meant."

As it happens, all of us were rather savvy in the Sondheim arena and were major fans of his work since the 1970s. Gary was entitled to his opinion, but when we learned that this was the first Sondheim musical he had ever seen, and because he spoke to us in an inflexible and patronizing tone, he'd lost all credibility. To spare our friend Kate's feelings, we maneuvered the conversation in another direction.

Over dessert the conversation had turned to the challenge of balancing the chore of walking one's dog each day with all of the other demands on one's time. We were all busy professionals, and although I have a yard in which to play with my two dogs, a couple of friends who lived in apartments spoke of their struggle to find time to take their beloved pooches on a robust daily romp.

Gary, apparently as much an expert on dogs as he was on Sondheim, chimed in, "People who live in apartments shouldn't own big dogs. They should have only small dogs, cats, or birds."

For a moment, the table fell silent. Then we spoke up. The debate escalated, and Gary never relented. He was so adamant in his beliefs that he couldn't hear a word of our case. No matter that the dogs in question were exercised daily or spent Saturdays with other dogs in a friend's large yard. We even pointed out that my friend's Rottweiler, Cupcake, was a rescue dog that would have been put to sleep if not taken in by my friend. No matter, Gary had dug in his heels, and the rest of us were dead wrong.

We got up from our coffee and dessert and fled. Kate let us know the next day that Gary was out of the picture.

Of course, there are also men out there who are worldly, well traveled, and well read. One type is deeply curious about the world and loves sharing and discussing his ideas. The other type, like Gary, simply wants an audience and the opportunity to show off.

Attractiveness

What's most attractive with this guy is that he often does know a lot about certain subjects. Anyone who becomes a pro at something can be a turn-on. His expertise speaks well of his discipline, commitment, and focus.

My husband, John, and I honeymooned in Paris. John is well versed in history and art and is an avid art collector. As we were sightseeing, he talked at length about the city and its past. He asked several times if he was talking too much. I told him absolutely not! I was enthralled by his stories and impressed by his learning. Because of John's insights and observations, I left France with a far greater appreciation for its art and culture.

Challenges

Unless you can influence *Mr. Know-It-All* to calm down and consider that other people also have valid perspectives, he will be difficult to live with. For him, seeing the merits of someone else's ideas is akin to him abdicating his throne, and he is unlikely to relinquish his expert title.

But if he's an otherwise great guy, he's not too terribly arrogant, and letting him be a *Know-It-All* doesn't bother you, this relationship might work. If you're the quiet type, his verboseness may be welcome. Bear in mind that your friends may not be as willing to tolerate him, and they might make themselves scarce.

Helpful Hints
Important questions to ask yourself:

1. Does he feel the need to act like an expert even when it's a subject he doesn't know much about? Does he always speak with an air of authority, even when it is not warranted? Does he embarrass you?
2. Does he interrupt you or others because he's so anxious to get in his two cents?
3. Do you feel heard when you speak, or do you feel judged and patronized?
4. Are you comfortable being the quiet one and letting him dominate the conversation?

Things to Do

In my experience, it is difficult to get these guys to calm down and become generous listeners. My best advice is to allow him to express himself, and then in your own words, tell him, "I heard you and appreciate your thoughts. May I have equal time now?" If he agrees and is actually open to hearing your comments, then repeat this until he learns that he cannot dominate the conversation without the people around him getting their chance to speak.

You also have the right to tell him, as we insisted with Gary, that you disagree with him. Adults are allowed to disagree. Ask to change the subject if he becomes too self-righteous. You don't have to defend your ideas and debate every subject of conversation.

If you are talking about something and he keeps interrupting or dismissing your ideas before you are finished, excuse yourself and end the conversation. The key is to not let arguments escalate. When necessary, let him know that the conversation is making you feel uncomfortable. Let him see that you don't wish to play along if he is going to be rude or bombastic.

It is possible he will grow to discover that the less argumentative and attached to his point he is, the more friends he will have. A *Mr. Know-It-All* who must be right and doesn't know how to listen or allow other points of view, risks ending up all alone. If your guy remains inflexible, you have the choice to live with it or leave. Only you will know what is right for you.

Epilogue

In Stephen Sondheim's musical, *Into the Woods*, Cinderella shares this bit of wisdom with Little Red Riding Hood:

> *Sometimes people leave you*
> *Halfway through the wood.*
> *Others may deceive you.*
> *You decide what's good.*

This insight comforts Little Red, and by the song's conclusion, the pair sing the refrain together:

> *You decide what's right,*
> *You decide what's good.*

In those two lines, Cinderella sums up the advice of this book. Relationships require effort. They require compromise. And yes, they most certainly present their own challenges, and at times you will feel hurt, alone, and uncertain.

But there is a vast difference between a relationship that feels like an endless struggle and one that has its rough patches.

I am the first to acknowledge that I also have fumbled in my relationships, felt blinded by the rush of romance, and only with time found the courage and clarity to leave a relationship that had no possibility of working. The problem isn't that we enter relationships that we later discover can't work, but that we stay in them to our detriment.

This book is about helping you gain clarity about men. Armed with this insight, you can determine whether the relationship meets your needs, can be made stronger, or is best abandoned for the promise of a fresh start. We should never be ashamed that finding a good relationship, like life, is a process of trial and error. The only thing that would be regrettable is if we didn't learn from our failed relationships.

Sondheim, who you might have guessed is my favorite composer and lyricist, poetically makes this very point in his musical, *Sunday in the Park with George*. The character Dot reflects on her failed relationship:

> *I chose, and my world was shaken*
> *So what?*
> *The choice may have been mistaken,*
> *The choosing was not.*
>
> *Just keep moving on.*

It's not the end of the world if things don't work out, or we made an effort and things didn't turn out as we had hoped. In my own experience, each relationship, from my first one in the third grade with Bill Brennan, to my marriage today, helped to make possible the relationship that followed. What gave me encouragement after my own bad break-ups was that I was choosing to take care of myself and making better choices about the men with whom I then got involved.

I couldn't help but notice that as my relationship with myself grew kinder and more loving, so too, did the men who showed up in my life.

While I might have portrayed in this book types of men who are not the best suited for loving and committed relationships, I did so in part to remind women that there is no good reason to be in a relationship with someone who doesn't think you are wonderful.

As my Sicilian grandmother would say, "*La vita e bella.*" Life is beautiful. In my own way, this is what I've written this book to tell you: Allow your life to be beautiful. Take a stand to find or create a relationship that brings you the most happiness, peace, and contentment. Treasure yourself, so it will feel like the most natural thing in the world when some guy comes along who truly treasures you.

Five years ago, I attended an elegant Christmas party for a friend's charity. From across the dimly lit room, I momentarily caught the eye of a man whose soulfulness shone like a lighthouse in the hazy blur of the crowd. Of course, I had no way of knowing in that instant that this man to whom I felt this sudden and powerful attraction would be the one. Just as in prior relationships, I had no way of knowing that those previous men were not going to be the one. But over the following months, that moment led to a wonderful courtship, engagement, and marriage.

How glad I am that some of those tougher, early relationships that cost me many tears hadn't dissuaded me from believing in love and taking another chance.

My wish for every woman who is reading this is to love yourself enough to only want what's best for you. The greatest things in life often come with growing pains. In *Into the Woods*, Cinderella reminds a discouraged Little Red Riding Hood that it's "Hard to see the light now. Just don't let it go."

I hope that this book leaves you feeling confident that you, too, know what feels right, and what feels good and what kind of man is most suitable for you.

About the Author

Catherine Cardinal, Ph.D., is the author of a Cure for the Common Life: The Cardinal Rules of Self-Esteem. Catherine is a Relationship Coach and creator of "The Cardinal Coaching Technique," a Movement Expression Therapist, and an Anger Management Facilitator. She is on staff at Rejuvalife Vitality Institute in Beverly Hills and The Stress and Anger Management Institute in Manhattan Beach.

Catherine Cardinal has appeared as an expert and relationship consultant on numerous television and radio shows, including *The O'Reilly Factor, Starting Over, Strange Universe, Good Day New York, Studio 2, Blind Date, KABC News, KCAL News, KCOP News,* and *WEWS News,* as well as the *Shirley MacLaine* and *Rolanda* radio programs.

She has also been cited as an expert in numerous publications, including the *Los Angeles Times, Glamour, Redbook, Maxim, Cosmopolitan, Modern Bride* as well as on Match.com.

Catherine is available for lectures and corporate trainings. For more information about her services, books, and speaking engagements, please visit www.catherinecardinal.com, or you can reach her by e-mail at: cc@catherinecardinal.com.

FREE AUDIO DOWNLOAD

Wise Women Get What They Want!

If you're ready to go to the next level in your life, personally or professionally, Catherine Cardinal's tried and true tools will help you take the next step. Listen as she shares valuable techniques that will help you realize your fullest potential. Learn how to use your innate wisdom to break through patterns that are stopping you from creating the life you want.

www.MenToRunFrom.com/FreeAudioDownload.html

A Cure for the Common Life:
The Cardinal Rules of Self-Esteem

A small but deceptively powerful book, *A Cure for the Common Life* pinpoints 10 specific ways to recognize the root cause of common problems and determine a realistic route for improvement. Written in a clear, thoughtful, heart-to-heart style, Catherine Cardinal's book gives you the confidence and support to finally take that giant leap – and make the changes you want in your life.

www.SelfEsteemDoc.com

Passion of One

This remarkable CD includes songs from some of the most inspired and diverse artists in the music industry. From rock to pop, to jazz and ballads, there will surely be a special song to invite and hold in your heart.

Listen to a sample at www.CatherineCardinal.com

Cardinal Coaching Technique

Catherine Cardinal offers effective, result oriented coaching sessions. Her expertise includes improving your self-esteem, decreasing anger and stress, dating and relationship advice and finding your creativity and passion. These can be done in person or over the phone.

For more information on The Cardinal Coaching Technique, please go to www.CatherineCardinal.com.

BUY A SHARE OF THE FUTURE IN YOUR COMMUNITY

These certificates make great holiday, graduation and birthday gifts that can be personalized with the recipient's name. The cost of one S.H.A.R.E. or one square foot is $54.17. The personalized certificate is suitable for framing and will state the number of shares purchased and the amount of each share, as well as the recipient's name. The home that you participate in "building" will last for many years and will continue to grow in value.

Here is a sample SHARE certificate:

YES, I WOULD LIKE TO HELP!

I support the work that Habitat for Humanity does and I want to be part of the excitement! As a donor, I will receive periodic updates on your construction activities but, more importantly, I know my gift will help a family in our community realize the dream of homeownership. **I would like to SHARE in your efforts against substandard housing in my community!** *(Please print below)*

PLEASE SEND ME _____ SHARES at $54.17 EACH = $ $_____

In Honor Of: _____

Occasion: (Circle One)   HOLIDAY   BIRTHDAY   ANNIVERSARY

      OTHER: _____

Address of Recipient: _____

Gift From: _____ *Donor Address:* _____

Donor Email: _____

I AM ENCLOSING A CHECK FOR $ $_____ PAYABLE TO HABITAT FOR HUMANITY **OR** PLEASE CHARGE MY VISA OR MASTERCARD *(CIRCLE ONE)*

Card Number _____ Expiration Date: _____

Name as it appears on Credit Card _____ Charge Amount $ _____

Signature _____

Billing Address _____

Telephone # Day _____ Eve _____

PLEASE NOTE: Your contribution is tax-deductible to the fullest extent allowed by law.
Habitat for Humanity • P.O. Box 1443 • Newport News, VA 23601 • 757-596-5553
www.HelpHabitatforHumanity.org

Printed in the United States
154045LV00004B/28/P